# IN THE
# AFTERMATH

What
September 11
Is Teaching Us
about Our World
Our Faith
& Ourselves

BOOKS BY JAMES TAYLOR

*Everyday Parables*

*Everyday Psalms*

*Letters to Stephen: A Father's Journey of Grief and Recovery*

*Precious Days & Practical Love: Caring for Your Aging Parent*

*Sin: A New Understanding of Virtue and Vice*

# IN THE
# AFTERMATH

**WHAT
SEPTEMBER 11
IS TEACHING US
ABOUT OUR
WORLD
OUR FAITH
& OURSELVES**

Edited by James Taylor

Northstone

Editors: James Taylor and Michael Schwartzentruber
Cover and interior design: Margaret Kyle
Proofreading: Dianne Greenslade


Northstone Publishing acknowledges the financial support of the Government of Canada
through the Book Publishing Industry Development Program for its publishing activities.

Northstone Publishing is an imprint of Wood Lake Books Inc., an employee-owned company, and is
committed to caring for the environment and all creation. Northstone recycles and reuses and encourages
readers to do the same. Resources are printed on recycled paper and more environmentally friendly
groundwood papers (newsprint), whenever possible. The trees used are replaced through donations to the
Scoutrees For Canada Program. A portion of all profit is donated to charitable organizations.

National Library of Canada Cataloguing in Publication Data
Main entry under title:
In the aftermath
ISBN 1-896836-56-9
1. September 11 Terrorist Attacks, 2001 – Religious aspects.
2. Terrorism – Religious aspects – Christianity.
3. September 11 Terrorist Attacks, 2001 – Psychological aspects.
I. Taylor, James, 1936-
HV6432.I57 2002     973.931     C2002-910596-X

Published by Northstone Publishing,
an imprint of Wood Lake Books Inc.
Kelowna, British Columbia, Canada

Printing 10 9 8 7 6 5 4 3 2 1
Printed in Canada at
Transcontinental Printing

# CONTENTS

# Foreword

When I returned from the 15th World Congress of International Physicians for the Prevention of Nuclear War in Washington, D.C., in early May, I received news that our organization had been chosen by the publishers to receive a portion of the revenues of this book. I was deeply touched and honored, but not completely surprised, to hear of this unsolicited act of generosity and support by a Canadian publisher. One of our outgoing co-presidents, Dr. Mary-Wynne Ashford, practices medicine in Victoria, B.C., and our Canadian affiliate, Physicians for Global Survival, has always been one of our strongest and most effective members. In case you have not heard about us, allow me to explain who we are and what we do.

International Physicians for the Prevention of Nuclear War is a global federation of 58 medical organizations founded to prevent nuclear war through research, education, and advocacy. Our member organizations work individually and in collaboration on programs promoting nonviolent conflict resolution, human rights, economic justice, and respect for our environment.

IPPNW began work in 1980, at the height of the Cold War, when a group of Soviet and American doctors met to sound a global warning about the medical reality of nuclear war. For their efforts, which reached millions with the message that nuclear weapons must never be used again, IPPNW received the 1985 Nobel Peace Prize. Today, IPPNW continues to unite people across political divides to prevent nuclear war.

Since September 11, 2001, we believe that the global threat posed by nuclear weapons has become more acute, immediate, and entrenched than ever. In May 2002, our World Congress in Washington, D.C., convened under the theme of "Summit for Survival." Washington had been selected as the congress site two years ago, when few could have imagined just how terribly appropriate this would be. As we met less than five miles from the Capitol, the U.S. Congress was in the process of appropriating money to fund the development of new types of nuclear weapons: "mini-nukes" and "bunker-busters." The crisis in the Middle East was at fever pitch and the mass media were predicting war with Iraq.

Still, in the midst of this crisis atmosphere, physicians and medical students from regional hot spots brought forth peaceful alternatives, including programs in the two areas of immediate danger: South Asia (where a nuclear exchange could take place with only four minutes lead time) and the Middle East. Activists from India, Pakistan, Bangladesh, and Nepal worked together in a spirit of positive and thoughtful cooperation. Physicians from Israel and Palestine shared their deep respect for human rights and nonviolent conflict resolution. Dr. Kenjiro Yokoro, who was a medical student at the University of Hiroshima when that city was destroyed by the world's first nuclear blast, was patiently teaching peace advocacy to doctors, medical students, and young activists. Dr. Yokoro has spent his entire life working to abolish nuclear weapons.

The contrast between *their* war fever and *our* peacemaking might have caused us to become self-satisfied. Fortunately, many veteran activists were there to remind us of how much more needed to be done. They reminded us that there is no *them*; there is only *us*. And that everyone, even peace activists, must learn from the events of September 11.

One great lesson we have learned is about the power of hope and of even the smallest and simplest acts of peacemaking in times of despair. In my work, I hear about these actions every day – over the Internet, by phone, by mail, in conversation. One person writes a letter about nuclear disarmament to the editor of her hometown newspaper in the United States. Another gives a talk about nuclear abolition at a meeting of physicians in Africa. A third marches in a demonstration against gun violence in Brazil. These acts seem small by themselves. Yet somehow, in some way, they all add up to more than we can ever imagine. They will, I believe, continue adding up and up until there really is peace – not just an absence of war. If not in my lifetime or my children's lifetime, then in the lifetime of generations to come.

Michael Christ
Executive Director of
International Physicians for the Prevention of Nuclear War

# 1

# Making a difference

## Derek Evans

One morning in September last year, I sat silently in front of a television with one of my sons, gripped by a moment that seemed to have no edges, no horizons of past or future, watching airplanes explode and skyscrapers collapse over and over again.

Gradually we began to develop a personal relationship with Tom, the TV announcer who struggled to give expression to our own confused feelings and confounded thoughts.

The day passed. Other children and their friends arrived home from school, where they had spent the day gathered in libraries and assembly halls sharing the same scenes. They grabbed snacks and joined us in the family room. On television, Tom searched for points of reference: Pearl Harbor? Kennedy?

Evening came. My son looked at me and asked, "Is this what history feels like?"

All heads turned away from the screen, and we looked at each other. Another young man spoke, "Yeah, I'm really trying to concentrate, because I think this is going to be our thing – where you're supposed to remember where you were and all that. But I'm not sure what I'm supposed to feel. Do you know how I'm supposed to feel?"

## A kind of unreality

The Al-Qaeda terrorist attacks on civilian targets in the United States were widely experienced, particularly in North America, as a sudden shock on many levels. At first, the dramatic quality and the extreme, vivid character of the attacks made them seem "unreal" to many people, as we observed them unfold in the midst of our daily lives and ordinary surroundings. On a more general social and cultural level, it became common to feel that "nothing would ever be the same again." It was as if we had become aware that we carried, deeply within our body politic, a serious, but undiagnosed, illness.

In the months since September 11, the economy seems to have begun slowly to "recover." But individuals, and North American society as a whole, appear to continue to be shaken, to be struggling to "make sense" of this newly defined reality. It may be that September 11, 2001, signaled the moment when many North Americans came to glimpse, and to some extent to share, the shape of life and the nature of reality that has been experienced by people in other parts of the world for many years.

Some suggested that the attacks represented the introduction of a new historical development – mass terrorism. But the brutal fact is that there is little new in this phenomenon, except that it has "come home" to North America. Various forms of mass and indiscriminate terrorism have been a significant feature of the daily experience of vast numbers of ordinary people in many parts of the world throughout the past century. No matter what the status or ideology of the perpetrator, whether clandestine group or state authority, and no matter what the culture or religion of the victim, the outcome has always been the same – the infliction of immeasurable suffering and grief upon millions of innocent people across the globe.

> The brutal fact is that there is little new in this phenomenon, except that it has "come home" to North America.

Is this new reality a nightmare from which we cannot escape? Or is it more as if we have just awakened, startled and disoriented, from a long sleep?

I believe it is the latter, and that belief gives me a ground for hope. It means we have the option to choose to not return to our slumbers – instead, to stay awake, to embrace the reality of the world that has opened before us, to assert an active role for ourselves and the values we care about within it.

Some say that in the years to come historians will look back on the 1990s as the "pre-war years." Distant and unreal as it may still seem, the fact is that our country is at war and our leaders have taken great pains to warn us that it will last for a long time.

For almost 20 years of my life, I was a kind of emergency worker in many – too many – situations of war, terrorism, and massive abuse. I have worked in Cambodia and Sri Lanka, in Colombia and Guatemala, in Sudan and South Africa, in Palestine and the Philippines, the former Yugoslavia, Russia, and many other places. I have seen enough of war to know that I hate war.

As people of faith, we know that evil is real and powerful. As people of faith, we also know that it can only be overcome by something equally real and even stronger – the transforming power of love. We know that revenge and retribution serve neither the cause of justice nor the call of compassion. We who are people of faith must speak and act on this truth.

Perhaps we need to consider how we will answer our children and grandchildren when they ask: "What did you do in the war?"

## The arrogance of explanations

On September 11, I continued to watch the television as Tom interviewed various experts who appeared as talking heads in separate frames on the screen. Each offered insight and opinions about who was responsible and what should be done. I was fascinated, in part, because Tom had similarly interviewed me a few times during the 1990s: once from Cambodia, once from Slovenia, and once from Sri Lanka, when I was an Amnesty International official conducting investigations into human rights atrocities. So, this is what it must have looked like!

On the screen, controversy had erupted. An academic at a Canadian university had dared to suggest that the cause of the terrorist attacks was rooted in the history of our policies and relations with the Islamic world, rather than being simply wanton acts of mindless wickedness committed by evil individuals. Although the notion that our society might share some responsibility for the situation seemed obvious and sensible enough to me, and though the academic seemed to bend over backwards to insist that this did not justify the attacks in any way, other commentators and experts rushed to repudiate and vilify her.

That messenger having been dealt with in the traditional manner, few others stepped forward to take her place.

Tom now assembled a new panel of experts. He introduced a collection of senior church leaders and asked them, "Why did God allow this to happen?"

I'm not sure what shocked me more: the fact that the archbishop in scarlet robes would attempt a lengthy explanation of why God would allow this to happen; or that we could conceive of everyone – evil individuals, whole nations of irrational people, even God – being responsible for this terrible situation except us!

Tom turned to a man in a dark suit with a glimmering glass cathedral in the background. "Pastor," he asked, "what would Jesus do?"

The minister clenched his fist and stared directly into the camera. "In this situation Jesus would insist that we *not* err on the side of mercy," he said. It was a forceful and moving statement, particularly in such a time of grief and confusing emotions. It may even have been a sincerely held belief on his part. But it was also an act of profound self-deception, the worst kind of lie.

I tried hard to imagine the possibility of Jesus, the prophet of the way of forgiveness, adopting such a posture. I felt grateful that I couldn't, and that the children had gone off to bed and missed this part of the discussion.

~
**I got up and turned off the television. In doing so, I felt that I was taking a first step back to reality.**
~

That's when I got up and turned off the television. In doing so, I felt that I was taking a first step back to reality. It was not that I was turning my back on the terrible events and the chain of consequences they had unleashed. Rather, I was refusing in one small way to take part in the great theatre of self-deception and scapegoating being offered as the way forward. I had begun to recognize the real "unreality" of the situation, and the sense of powerlessness it engenders.

## Neither unspeakable nor unthinkable

Often, during these days and months following September 11, I have heard the atrocities described as "unspeakable." Yet almost always this description has been a prelude to the speaking of many words – like "reprisal," "retaliation," even "revenge" – that seemed designed to reinforce the idea of evil being located in some distant place where it could be "hunted down."

During these days and months I have also heard the acts of terrorism described as "unimaginable." Yet any of us who have observed our children's video games, scanned the listings of popular movies, or looked deeply and honestly into our own hearts, know to our shame that there is nothing in these events that is altogether alien to us or to the spirit of our society and its sometimes twisted fantasies.

I believe that "reality" begins when we start putting ourselves back in the picture. We begin to regain a sense of our own power when we stop giving it away to those who are not trustworthy, and instead start to try to understand and take responsibility for our own place in the world.

## Learning from successes

We are generally encouraged to learn from our mistakes, but I think we rarely do so. Or perhaps we just learn the wrong sorts of things from them. In most organizations, we focus on failure. We see mistakes as failures. The main thing we learn is how to make excuses, apportion blame, and avoid responsibility. These may be valid survival tactics. But they do not necessarily teach us how to thrive or to move forward together.

I've become convinced that it is more important to try to learn from success, to draw energy from our positive experiences that can be applied to other situations.

During the past century, successes may have been few, fragile, and fleeting. But there are some, and from them we can draw positive learnings about how to respond appropriately and effectively to violence and terrorism. If we choose to learn from success rather than simply react to failure, then situations around the world suggest a very few pragmatic but essential elements that might serve as guides for us as we seek to create a new future. Whether it is confronting deeply rooted hatred and trauma in South Africa or Chile, or attempting to reconstruct a society from complete devastation in Cambodia or Timor, or the determination of the mothers of Argentina and elsewhere to obtain the truth, or attempting to overcome barriers between communities in Ireland, Sri Lanka, or Canada, our experiences point to the importance of one basic starting point – taking responsibility for our own part in both the problem and the solution.

## The discipline of self-criticism

That means, first of all, developing and exercising the discipline of self-examination. We must focus on what we can do or need to do to address a situation, rather than being preoccupied with defining what we expect others to do.

For many years my work regularly involved meeting with heads of state or members of the cabinets of governments around the world, to confront them with documented complaints of human rights violations in their country and to persuade them to correct the situation and prevent future occurrences. These negotiations were usually very tense and difficult. They tended to follow a typical pattern. Government officials would usually deny the accuracy of our information. Then they challenged the legitimacy of our motives and sources. Sometimes they even attempted to threaten us in some manner. The extent and severity of these stages varied from one government to another, but only after they had been formally dealt with could we hope to work practically and constructively on the actual concerns.

Another stage in the process invariably appeared, that seemed to be more instinctive than tactical. In all cases, the government would insist on discussing the alleged violations of those with whom they were in competition or conflict – the insurgents or terrorist groups, neighboring countries or other enemies. I was struck that, in most cases, political leaders had a much more intimate knowledge of what their enemy had done, and a clearer vision of what their enemy should do to improve the situation, than they had of their own practices and responsibilities. The information we presented about their own country's record often came as a sincere surprise to them.

I also found that the deeper and more persistent was their need to focus on the perceived wrongs and responsibilities of the other party, the more intractable their own violation of basic human rights would be, and the less likely any prospect of change.

## Acting our values

Another implication of taking responsibility for our own roles is that we need to accept that the values and qualities we want to see reflected in our lives, and in our world, will never appear as some magical gift. They are, rather, a direct result of our commitment and determination to act in ways that produce those values. Values are not simply attitudes we "hold" like possessions. Nor are they simply ideas that guide our behavior or shape our policies. Especially, they are not a set of mysterious but intangible factors, like the "chemistry" of personal attraction, that are either present in a situation or not.

> We create values through our actions, deliberate or otherwise.

We create values through our actions, deliberate or otherwise. And they have real effect. Values are the powerful, practical means by which we can contribute to changing the world through intentional, consistent, and determined action.

Most of us know all this, of course. But far too often we act as if we believe otherwise.

Any of us who are parents, or children, know that values and qualities of the home environment in which we grow up have powerful effects on our personalities and potentialities. Yet in our institutions and in society we often ignore this wisdom and succumb to mystification. If there is a lack of trust in an organization, for example, we may fatalistically treat it as normal. We may accommodate ourselves to living with the results. We may bemoan the lack of trust to justify other problems. Yet we know that certain actions can increase the level of trust: such as by providing opportunities for people to be listened to, showing that we are willing to learn from others, making information available, demonstrating that policies will be followed, openly acknowledging when mistakes happen and taking steps to correct or prevent them, and so on.

If we want more trust in our world, if we ourselves want to be trusted, then we ourselves need to be trustworthy. Yet too rarely in our social, organizational, or political lives do we take up the challenge of actually creating the value we care about by defining and practicing the behaviors that will both express and produce it.

The notion that we can create values by acting to produce them provides me with a real basis for hope. It supports the possibility of believing that we – each of us – matter; and that together we can make a meaningful difference in the world. I am continually struck by the extent to which this is what people, particularly young people, are craving – the confidence that we matter, and the jealous determination to find ways to make a difference.

So much in our society conspires to deny that belief. So much is arranged to persuade us of our own futility and powerlessness, of the irrelevance or utter relativism of our values and beliefs. One of the key challenges of taking responsibility is to begin to take ourselves seriously, to behave as if what we do really matters.

## Signs of progress

Taking ourselves seriously is a revolutionary act; it takes deliberate effort. I am not referring to egotism or self-absorption, or even to self-esteem. By taking ourselves seriously I mean recognizing that we not only have values, we also create them – indeed, that we have both the responsibility and the power to make them real.

I believe this is possible because I have experienced it. Most of the instruments we have developed to promote peace and justice at the international level – whether as treaties and standards like the Universal Declaration on Human Rights and the Convention Against Torture or as organizations like Amnesty International and Médecins Sans Frontières – have come into existence as a result of the caring and determined efforts of a few individuals who took themselves and their values seriously.

The same is true, more recently, for the initiative to ban landmines and the treaty to create an International Criminal Court to bring an end to impunity for crimes against humanity. Amnesty's experience in investigating human rights abuses for more than 40 years is that the single most important factor in perpetuating violations is the confidence of the perpetrators that they will not be brought to justice.

> Most of the instruments we have developed to promote peace and justice...have come into existence as a result of the caring and determined efforts of a few individuals who took themselves and their values seriously.

Although several previous efforts to establish an international court had failed, and although conventional wisdom held that such a court was not politically possible, a handful of committed individuals decided in the early 1990s to learn from our successes and to create public impetus demanding the creation of an international court. That handful of individuals became a network of small groups throughout the world who drafted the legislation, lobbied governments to convene a treaty conference, and mobilized public opinion to demand agreement. Within only a few years, a UN treaty in 1998 established the basis for an International Criminal Court, to come into effect once 60 countries voted to ratify the agreement. By the end of April 2002, more than 66 nations had signed on, and the court came into effect on July 1, 2002. Significantly the United States still opposes it, fearing that some of its own citizens, former leaders, and political allies might be among the first to face indictment for acts of international terrorism and crimes against humanity.

If we truly seek to assert and defend certain values – such as our dedication to democracy, human rights, the rule of law, and internationalism – we must be rigorous and consistent in our own adherence to those values. While I believe we should oppose terrorism, even in some cases through military action, we must ensure that we oppose all those who practice terrorism. That is, not just those who see us as their enemy, but also those – including sympathetic governments – who use terrorism to support causes we may favor.

We should denounce any acts that appear to be motivated by revenge or discrimination. We should insist that any military action carried out in the name of justice is directed by international agencies and accountable to international law. We should encourage the strengthening of institutions that support justice and accountability for both friends and enemies, especially the International Criminal Court.

## Understanding the causes

One of the most difficult aspects of taking responsibility for our part in the problem and the solution is trying to understand the cause. This is especially hard in a situation of mass terrorism, when our fear and legitimate sense of outrage make listening almost impossible.

Even at the best of times, however, understanding the cause represents a major challenge. It requires an attentiveness to historical context. Especially in North America, we tend not to remember events even when they are regularly present in our lives and culture. For example, we've all seen enough war movies that many of us, even in Canada, can probably sing the first line of the U.S. Marine Corps anthem – "*From the halls of Montezuma, to the shores of Tripoli…*" But I suspect few, even in the United States, could explain what is it all about! "Montezuma" is clear enough, an intervention in Mexico. But "Tripoli" refers to an incident about two hundred years ago when the Marines were sent to attack Muslim communities in the part of North Africa that is now Libya. The purpose was to eradicate state-sponsored piracy in the Mediterranean – the main terrorist threat to international trade at the time. It makes you wonder whether how much really changed on September 11!

# Ignoring history

While I was in Vancouver for a few days recently, I arranged to have breakfast one morning with my friend Geoff. We get together now and again to catch up on family matters and to solve the problems of the world. We don't do it often enough (obviously!), because he travels a great deal as a consultant for World Bank projects. This time, soon after September 11, we agreed on achieving peace in the Middle East before we examined the restaurant's menu.

Most of the breakfast options involved croissants with different fillings. I commented on how appropriate that seemed, given our topic. Geoff looked puzzled.

I suspect that few people in the restaurant that morning would remember the significance of 1683 from their world history class in high school, even though it is a key date in Western history. Indeed, it continues to affect the lives of thousands of Canadians every day – those who serve as peacekeepers in Bosnia or Kosovo, those who investigate mass graves or prosecute war criminals, and those who assist refugees from those places. In fact, we connect with it every time we eat a croissant – a treat invented to celebrate the defeat of the Muslims at the gates of Vienna just over three hundred years ago, and the beginning of the attempt to eliminate the presence of Islam in Europe. In a sense, the wars in the former Yugoslavia in the 1990s were echoes or "mopping up" operations from that event.

The crescent is a symbol of Islam – as the cross is to Christianity – and the appearance of the crescent-shaped pastry in Western cuisine was originally a way of celebrating their destruction. Be careful what snacks you serve at an interfaith event!

Most people have never realized that the Western world has been at war with the Islamic world for more than a thousand years. I believe this lack of recognition in itself is significant, and worth some reflection.

Our lack of awareness is not simply because we are bad at history; it touches on the nature of history itself. We tend to look at the world and history from the perspective of the winners. Our lack of awareness of these historical events reflects the prerogative of the victor to refuse to recognize even the existence of a conflict or of its victims. So we ask, bewildered, "What war? What victims? Why do these people hate us so much? What is *their* problem?"

## Not a new conflict

If we were asked to describe the historical war between Islam and the West, most of us would automatically refer to the Crusades, and probably only to that one episode from the distant past. I suspect we remember only that part of the story because that is the time when "our side" lost. If we tend to remember our defeats, our humiliations, our suffering, we should not expect it to be different for other people. In seeking to understand Islam, and the relation between Islam and the West – including acts of terrorism – we need to begin with the recognition that we have long been peoples at war with each other, and that they have much more pain to remember than we do.

> Understanding the cause of others' behavior or motivation usually turns out to involve a need to better understand my own.

If Geoff and I had been sitting in a café in Beirut or Baghdad, Cairo or Kabul, I suspect that many of the people having breakfast could have told us what happened in 1683 — that is, aside from the invention of the croissant.

It should not be surprising that we find it so difficult to understand other cultures or faiths, such as Islam, when most of us know so little about our own. In fact, in my experience, understanding the cause of others' behavior or motivation usually turns out to involve a need to better understand my own. That is certainly the case when it comes to the relation between the Western nations and the Islamic world. Though it has been an extremely intimate relationship, we have been outsiders to each other for over a thousand years. We have shared a history, a book, and even, to a large extent, a holy place. But our experiences, and how we remember them, have been very different.

If I asked the people having breakfast at that Vancouver café to name the most significant dates in world history of the past millennium, I suspect their answers would deal with "our" history, probably with little or no reference to Islam. If we were to ask the patrons of the café in a Muslim country the same question, some dates might be the same, some different. However, I suspect that "their" dates would mostly be very much about their relationship to us, though they might refer to events we barely remember.

## The relevance of Islam

Understanding the cause of extreme behaviors such as terrorist acts can be hard work. As a general approach, one practical way is to start from an assumption that others are acting on the basis of some real, felt concern. It is also useful to start from an assumption that the cause will probably not be found either in them or in us, but rather within the character of our relationship. Although the attitudes of terrorists or other ideologically motivated groups may seem irrational, there is almost always some grain of legitimate grievance at the root of their protest. While I do not in any way suggest that terrorist acts should in any way be condoned or justified, our failure to recognize and address the root causes perpetuates terrorism, instead of eliminating it.

Understanding the cause is a challenge we might well exercise in broader issues as well. To guide us, for example, in developing serious approaches to interfaith dialogue. Although many people may associate "Islam" mainly with "terrorism" or "fundamentalism," Islam is the fastest growing religion in the world, including throughout Europe and North America. Why? I will leave it to others to define this faith tradition historically, or to explain its intrinsic spiritual power. But it may be useful to try to ask what it is about Islam that makes it so appealing to so many people in so much of the world today.

From my perspective, a number of observations emerge.

First, Islam offers a disciplined approach to personal and collective life, clearly rooted in spiritual practice. There is a real hunger for that in a world that seems for many people to be increasingly out of control, out of meaning.

Second, aside from Quakerism, Islam is in many ways the most egalitarian and democratic of organized religions. Most of Islam has no established religious hierarchy. The word "imam" is often translated as "priest," but it literally means simply "prayer leader." Individuals are responsible for their religious faithfulness, and all share the same obligations. In the essential posture of Islam, each person stands (or bows) before God not as a member or representative of anything, not even as a believer, but simply as a human being. There is a real hunger for that in a world in which many feel increasingly lost among the consuming and competing masses.

Third, Islam is compelling because it offers a real sense of solidarity. We can't understand Judaism if we don't remember that, in its origins, it is "the religion of refugees and strangers" – offering fundamentally a sense of home, family, and destiny. The philosopher Simone Weil once described Christianity, approvingly, as "the religion of slaves." To a large extent, Christianity grew as a vibrant, global religion not because it offered an "opiate to the masses," as Marx claimed, but because it offered respect, integrity, freedom and community, human dignity and wholeness, to the slaves of the Roman Empire. If Christians forget that aspect of their origins, they lose touch with the heart of their faith. Perhaps the Romans should have tried to learn from it, rather than just trying to repress it.

I believe that in our day, whether we like it or not, Islam is the "religion of the oppressed." In a world increasingly dominated by corporate arrogance and superpower unilateralism, Islam offers many people a refuge, a place of resistance, and a language of defiance. There is a real hunger for that. Perhaps, like the Romans, we should try to learn from it rather than simply react to it in ignorance or fear.

If dealing with terrorism must be accepted as a major feature of the political landscape for the foreseeable future, it is important for us to take action now to create the future we hope for, and the relationships that will be its foundation. We should assist the development of civil society in Afghanistan and elsewhere. We should encourage community, support nongovernmental organizations and other agencies that promote and protect human rights – even if they say and do things that make us uncomfortable. In the long run, our own security, as well as the security of Afghan and other peoples, will depend more on aid, assistance, and cooperation than on spies, intelligence, and control.

Remember, we are more likely to create the future we really want if we start living it, if we start investing in the relationships and values we care about, now!

> **We are more likely to create the future we really want if we start living it.**

## Unexpected legacy of the Cold War

For most of humanity, the world really did change in significant ways following the collapse of another symbolic structure of Western architecture – the Berlin Wall – in 1989. The end of the Cold War created a new political environment. It gave us a vital opportunity to remove the ideological barrier that had provided a great excuse for not implementing justice and peace, respecting human rights, and creating a safer and healthier world for all.

In some ways, the "peace dividend" did create a framework for fulfilling these hopes. In the field of human rights, for example, a range of positive measures were initiated. The UN and other international agencies were reformed on the basis of "human rights mainstreaming" and the strengthening of civil society. The Universal Declaration of Human Rights was formally renewed (the Vienna Declaration), and a practical plan for implementing it was developed. There was also an international commitment to the promotion and protection of the rights of women (Beijing Action Plan); a movement towards addressing impunity, through the creation of an International Criminal Court (Statute of Rome); and the establishment of an infrastructure to support the role of human rights defenders (General Assembly Declaration). The international community began to open up important new fields for debate and policy-making, such as the responsibility and accountability of businesses, corporations, armed opposition groups, and others for the promotion of human rights and the protection of the environment.

The end of the Cold War also meant, however, that whole regions of the world – notably Africa and Central Asia – ceased overnight to hold any strategic interest for those with political and economic power. They were summarily marginalized, then abandoned. Just as suddenly, warlords and dictators who had served as superpower surrogates – created, sponsored, and largely controlled by either the Soviet Union or the West – were loosed upon their countries to pursue their own interests without restraint. Some acted as agents of convenience for big corporations and other forces of globalization in an increasingly unregulated and competitive world.

Although the "cold" international struggle was over, the number of "hot" domestic conflicts proliferated from about 30 to more than 80 within the first five years of the decade.

From a human rights perspective, these developments significantly changed the nature and scale of violations experienced by ordinary people around the world. Individuals were no longer targeted primarily by repressive governments because of their ideological beliefs or political involvements and punished with arbitrary imprisonment and torture. During the 1990s, human rights violations changed from repression of beliefs to an assault on identities – whether gender, language, religion, or ethnicity.

> Instead of attempting to control their enemies, human rights violators increasingly sought to eliminate them.

In the wars that increasingly defined the lives of more and more people, the key question changed from being "What side are you on?" to simply "Who are you?" Instead of attempting to control their enemies, human rights violators increasingly sought to eliminate them. The same forms of mass terrorism that international human rights law was created to ensure would "never again" be part of the human experience, erupted once more all around the world: genocide in Central Africa, ethnic cleansing in Eastern Europe, slavery of women and children in large parts of Africa and

Asia. For most people in most of the world, despite great efforts and many achievements, the world was a much harsher and more dangerous place at the end of the 1990s than it had been at the beginning.

## A dawning of awareness

After turning off the television, I began reflecting on my own glimpses of mass terrorism. I remembered the stories that Tom had interviewed me about during my years as one of those talking-head experts.

The first time had been when I was in Cambodia, a country devastated by decades of horror – the years of bombing by the United States, the massive social purges of the Khmer Rouge, and finally invasion and occupation by the Vietnamese. Peace negotiations had finally resulted in an agreement among the warring factions to create a new way forward, and a commitment by the international community to support the rebuilding of the country.

I was in the country to meet with members of the new government to assist in making human rights an integral part of the process.

In some ways it felt as if we were starting from the very beginning. As part of their project of creating a brand new communist society, the Khmer Rouge had attempted to wipe out all vestiges of the previous system – even if it meant killing everyone who could read or wore glasses. One of my first meetings was to be with the members of the Supreme Court, except that no one knew where I might find them. After a day of following up all kinds of leads, I finally found an old man sitting beside a filing cabinet beneath a shady tree in someone's back garden. He was the Supreme Court.

In other ways it felt as if we were confronting an unending legacy of violence and abuse. I was scheduled to meet with the Minister of National Security, but my transportation had disappeared. No one in the crowd of taxi drivers and guides who gathered to help me at the main intersection of downtown Phnom Penh knew who that Minister was, or where I could find him. Finally I said, "Take me to the place of the bad police." Everyone automatically knew exactly where to go. In a few minutes a convoy of taxis pulled up in front of a massive wall bearing large stainless steel lettering: "Department of National Security and Public Safety."

Behind the wall, after my meeting, I encountered a man who had been arrested in one of the outlying villages for some small infraction. A peasant, he had clearly been beaten at some point in the process. I began to interview him to obtain details and offer assistance.

> Once we embrace our humanity and claim our inherent dignity, there is no going back.

After a few exchanges, he looked confused and asked me, "Sir, why are you asking me these questions? Is something wrong?"

It was my turn to feel confused. I said, "Well, sir, it appears to me that you have been beaten by the police."

The man realized he was speaking to a fool. He spoke with great patience, as if explaining how to add two plus two: "Of course, they are the police and I am a peasant. They caught me and so I was beaten. That is how it is, how it always has been."

Our discussion continued for some time. In one of the truly privileged moments of my life, I saw this man come to the realization that the notion of "human" rights included him.

And in that moment I too learned something. About change. Once we embrace our humanity and claim our inherent dignity, there is no going back. Grave violations of human rights – torture, indiscriminate killings, the acts of mass terrorism – will certainly continue to occur, in many situations with increasing severity. But there is now almost no corner of the world where even the poorest and most marginalized people do not know and believe that their oppression is not deserved, is not their due, and is wrong.

I believe this global awareness is one of the great achievements of the last decades. Though largely unrecognized, I believe it represents both a revolutionary change and a real basis for hope. It expresses the bond that unites us. It creates the ground upon which we might commit ourselves to ensuring that it is realized for each other – to create the values we know to be right.

When our protests secured the release of that man, when I watched him return home to his family, I knew I was witnessing the birth of a new future.

## No easy answers

The second time Tom contacted me from his studio I was in the country that used to be Yugoslavia. The wars in Slovenia, Croatia, and Bosnia had been staunched, for the moment at least; the wars in Kosovo, Serbia, and Macedonia were still to come. A number of us were concerned that there were few signs of the emergence of a domestic movement for peace and justice in the region, the kinds of civil society initiatives that are essential to the creation of any real basis for social change.

In other situations of social trauma around the world, in Argentina or Guatemala for example, groups of women like the Mothers of the Disappeared had acted as catalysts, generating courage and commitment to human rights throughout their communities. It seemed that their common identity and experience, as women who had suffered a loss of a loved one, enabled them to transcend differences of class, race, or ideology.

We thought that bringing together women from the various ethnic groups who had lost a loved one in the civil wars might spur the development of a human rights movement in the region.

It was too easy a solution. One of my teachers was the late Jack Shaver. He would regularly shake his finger at me and shout such things as "The helping hand strikes again!" or "There is no mission without permission!" In the former Yugoslavia I began to understand that "learning from success" takes practice!

We brought a hundred women together for a weekend. Almost immediately things began to fall apart. After my welcoming address, participants from Serbia and Croatia began to insist on translation in order to understand each other. At first I assumed these were tactical gambits, to score points to satisfy the political authorities at home. After all, for most of their lives, all of these women had spoken a language officially known as Serbo-Croat. But soon I realized that they were sincere. The divisions between their communities were so deep, the sense of each being the victim of the other so profound, that they really were unable to understand each other, despite knowing the same language.

I came away from that experience with an understanding that no one can empower or liberate another. At best we can create conditions to make transformations possible, by removing any obstacles or impediments that we may have put in the way.

> I came away from that experience with an understanding that no one can empower or liberate another. At best we can create conditions to make transformations possible.

But I also came away with a sense of the importance and urgency, for all of us, of learning the language and practice of reconciliation. Indeed, I have come to believe that this is one of the primary challenges we face as a species, a key to understanding how we create a viable and sustainable future.

## Breaking the cycle

In the almost 60 years since the Holocaust, a substantial body of research has been built up concerning how survivors cope with and are affected by situations of severe trauma. Individuals who have suffered from extreme violence, such as torture, often have had so much of their human dignity stripped from them that they may come to believe that all they have left is their identity as a victim. They may begin to define their very identity by their relation to the perpetrator. Sometimes they even cling desperately to this relationship in the fear that without it they will have, or be, nothing but their pain.

In the former Yugoslavia I came to see that this dynamic operates on a social and community level as well. Although absolutely vital in the immediate term, I am concerned that many of our efforts at peace-keeping, conflict resolution, and mediation may in the longer term reinforce and even perpetuate these problems, because they are based on defining the terms of separation of those who have been in conflict, rather than establishing the basis of their future relationship.

In an increasingly globalized world, separation and isolation are luxuries that we cannot afford. Whether in the former Yugoslavia, in Central Africa, in the Middle East, in the relations between the West and Islam, or in our own communities, we need to learn how to practice reconciliation. Reconciliation begins, I believe, when we recognize that, whether we like it or not, we are in each other's future. Practicing reconciliation requires that we find a way to break free of our perceived roles as victim or perpetrator, and build our relationship on a new foundation – one that is based on our authentic identities.

> **Practicing reconciliation requires that we find a way to break free of our perceived roles as victim or perpetrator.**

Learning the way of reconciliation is an urgent task. It will require the risk of experimentation. But if there is to be a long term, we have no choice. Learning the way of reconciliation is the discipline of being present to the future, rather than being bound to the past.

Another thing we have learned from research on violent trauma is that persons who have been tortured experience and express specific behavioral dysfunctions. If they are not dealt with effectively, these behaviors are transferred within family and community systems for at least four generations. This is true even in situations where there has been no direct contact between the ones who experienced the torture and the later generations. We know it is at least four generations because that is the current extent of the research base, but it is probably much longer. In a world characterized by mass terrorism, it is urgent that we learn how to break the cycle of perceived mutual victimization before it perpetuates itself, yet again.

## Refusing to give up

The last time I was interviewed by Tom was in Sri Lanka, while the civil war that had simmered and boiled intermittently for the past three decades was raging. Terrible atrocities were being committed on all sides. For most people, every sunset ushered in a time of unbounded fear and, for some, the deepest horror. The government of the time had declared Amnesty International a "terrorist organization." A very active death squad had issued a threat over the public media against my delegation. Our status made the danger we faced "newsworthy," and Tom wanted to pursue that story. Other messages that we received during that visit seemed to touch more deeply the reality of the situation, but I could find no way to convey that to Tom at the time.

Embelipitiya is a small town in the south of Sri Lanka, filled with respectable, well educated, middle-class people of the majority culture. But the civil war had taken hold there as well. Special troops were sent with orders to suppress the insurgency, and the commander met with the local political leaders. Together they came to a coldly rational conclusion. They instructed the high school teachers to provide lists of the ten best students in each of the senior classes, on the logical assumption that the brightest of the young people would be most likely to criticize the government and cause trouble. Over the next three nights, after darkness fell, the military collected the 40 young people on the lists from their homes – in many cases, tearing them from the arms of their parents.

For a few days the young people were kept under arrest at the military camp. Their parents could sometimes glimpse them through a fence, or when the gate opened for a moment. But one night the soldiers broke camp and moved on. The children were nowhere to be found. The parents searched. They made enquiries everywhere – until officials advised them to stop asking questions or they and their other children might also go missing.

The day after we arrived in the country, a stranger came to see us with a message from the parents of those children who had "disappeared." They asked us to come to their town. I knew that the government and the military were watching my delegation closely, so I sent a message back saying it would not be possible. It would take a day and a night to reach their town from the capital; there were military checkpoints on all the highways; anyone seen in contact with my delegation would be in great danger. So I put it out of my mind, and we went on with our work.

A couple of days later, as I walked down the street, someone slipped another message into my pocket. It asked me to come later that night to a church around the corner from my hotel. When it was dark, a colleague and I slipped out for a walk. The church looked shut and empty. We found the door unlocked, stepped into the silent sanctuary, and closed the door behind us. After a moment a match was struck, and a candle lit, then another and another, until the church seemed full of light. As the light grew, I realized it was also full of people, the parents and grandparents and brothers and sisters of those disappeared young people. The cold and lonely sanctuary became a living, sacred place.

Although they were very afraid, those family members were so full of love for their lost children, and so filled with a hunger for the truth and a determination for justice, that their hearts had no room left for fear. Although I knew that I was in the presence of a sorrow so deep and a grief so raw that I could not pretend to grasp it, at the same time I felt that I had never touched such an overflowing of caring and love, of compassion and determination. I sensed the very spirit of life, power, and freedom.

We worked together with those families for the next ten years. Three governments came and went, but the care and commitment of the families, and their dedication to truth and justice, persisted. We succeeded in identifying the main perpetrators of the abuses, pursued prosecutions against them through the courts, and eventually won convictions for most of those responsible – senior military officers and a high school principal. We trained a cadre of forensic investigators and exhumed numerous mass graves. The remains of many children were recovered but, to this point, not those of the families of Embelipitiya.

## Keeping our hearts open

Among all the thousands of "cases" I worked on during my years with Amnesty International, I think I cared most deeply about this one. I think it is because, through they had much cause, the families seemed never to be motivated by a sense of bitterness or vengeance, but only by their love – for their children, for each other, for the hope of a healthy future for their country.

> The discipline of the open heart means that we will inevitably experience hurt.

Perhaps the most important aspect, and challenge, of taking responsibility in a world of mass terrorism is this determination to keep open not only our minds and hands, but also our hearts. It is difficult, because it means remaining open, even if it is possible only in some small measure, to sharing the pain of those we seek to understand, of those with whom we seek to be in solidarity. The root of the word "compassion" means to "suffer with." So the discipline of the open heart means that we will inevitably experience hurt, and even a certain scarring in our work.

The great paradox and mystery of our experience, one that often appears at the core of our understanding of spirituality, is that it is precisely in this act of embracing the suffering of another that we may discover a special strength, the possibility of healing, even grace.

# 2

# The Christian response to violence

## Stanley Hauerwas

I am a representative of Christian nonviolence.

For me, a person seldom at a loss for words, I find my continuing reaction to September 11, 2001, to be one of silence. I simply do not know what to say. At least one of the reasons I have nothing to say is because I am a pacifist. I am, whether I like it or not, committed to Christian nonviolence. Yet the horror, the terror, the strange beauty of the flames and the dust and the violence on September 11, calls for a response, even a violent response. Being a pacifist does nothing to free me from the desire to set things right by punishing those who perpetrated such an outrage.

Conflicted, I am tempted to remain silent, fearing any words I may say would suggest a confidence I do not have.

Often people think a pacifist has nothing to say other than, "War is bad and this one is bad too." I suggest that Christian nonviolence – at least the Christian nonviolence I have learned from John Howard Yoder – has some things to say to help us understand better what is confronting us in the aftermath of September 11, 2001.

For Christians, September 11, 2001, is not the day that changed our world. The world, the cosmos, what we call history, was changed in 33 A.D. Anything we say after September 11, 2001, requires that what happened on September 11, 2001, be narrated in the light of the birth, death, and resurrection of the person we know as the Christ.

To reduce the consideration of our response to the simplistic question, "What would Jesus do?" is either stupid or dishonest. Nor is the real question, "What would Jesus *have* us do?" The real question is how we should live given what God has already done through the cross and resurrection of Jesus Christ.

I do not believe that pacifist and just war advocates must necessarily answer that question differently. Christian advocates of nonviolence and of just war both believe that through the cross and resurrection we have been given the time, the patience, faithfully to follow Christ by refusing to use evil means in the name of a good cause.

## Dismissal of pacifism

In the aftermath of September 11, pacifism has had a rough ride. The editors of a journal of whose editorial board I am a member wrote an editorial entitled "In Time of War." In it, they stated: "Those who in principle oppose the use of military force have no legitimate part in the discussion about how military force should be used."

The editorial took for granted, without question, the Niebuhrian distinction between nonviolent resistance and non-resistance. Niebuhr, you may remember, made that distinction based on his understanding of politics. Niebuhr was quite clear: Jesus was an advocate of non-resistance. Therefore, he argued, Christians must leave Jesus behind when they come to the political realm. They must do so because politics, by his definition, is disguised violence. The best one can hope for in politics is the most equitable balance of power. At best, Jesus' ethic of love stands as a judgment on every accomplishment of justice. But any attempt to realize the disinterested love symbolized by the cross in politics indulges in utopianism that only makes politics more violent.

John Howard Yoder spent a lifetime trying to convince Mennonites they should not accept the Niebuhrian "compliment" – i.e., that absolute pacifists are to be admired only if they acknowledge they are politically irresponsible. In essay after essay and book after book, Yoder patiently developed a Christological account of Christian nonviolence that rejected the Niebuhrian distinction – a distinction that has no exegetical basis – between nonviolent resistance and nonresistance.

Even the title of his book, *The Politics of Jesus,* is a clear rebuttal of the Niebuhrian attempt to make Jesus' "ethic" nonpolitical.

## The difference between unity and community

One of the things confronting us (if you ever wanted, really wanted, to know what "political correctness" is) is that we are now living in a time when political correctness has become obligatory. Those who express any concern about the American response to September 11 are assumed to bear the burden of proof. That is real political correctness.

That we live at a time of such political correctness is partly because Americans have suddenly found community. We have been united by opposition to a perceived enemy. The fact that this enemy is as much created as real, and that the president of this nation has exploited this opposition to build his own personal popularity to unprecedented levels, is one of the elements that political correctness prohibits us from discussing.

> Americans have suddenly found community. We have been united by opposition to a perceived enemy.

The new sense of unity that Americans seem to feel after September 11, 2001, is surely a judgment on the church. Unity is what we are about as Christians. Eucharist is the feast of unity. That Christians find themselves instead captured by the unity offered by the flag is surely a sign that we who are the church have been less than God called us to be.

What a horror it would be if this nation must be morally renewed by war. Is the American response to September 11 a confirmation of Hegel's suggestion that bourgeois states periodically need to be renewed through war?

I am often supposed to be for community. Thus I have been described as a sectarian fideistic tribalist. The use of "tribalist" means that I am considered a communitarian. I always say I'm not a communitarian: I'm a Christian. I'm not a communitarian because communitarianism in America, against the background of a liberal society, always means nationalism. The "we" that is constructed in nationalism means that people suddenly find themselves in unity across class, race, and ethnic divides and this is extremely dangerous. Hopefully the "we" won't be any deeper a loyalty than that we give to a pro football team. However, how this rediscovery of the "we" is used could be extremely dangerous.

There is very little space in our present society for anyone to attempt to step back and ask, "Why do these people hate us?" To ask, "Do you think they attacked the World Trade Center because they hate American freedoms?" is again a question that cannot be raised. If you say, as one entertainer did, "Well, it doesn't look to me like those people were cowards. I think cowards are people that set off missiles from the middle of the ocean to attack civilians," then you are not heard on the air at all.

These reactions are understandable, given the horror of the attack on the World Trade Center. But we need a space to get our breaths. I like to think that the commitment to Christian nonviolence can help us to create that space.

> ~
> The church to which I belong seems captured by the identification of God and country.
> ~

## Identifying God with country

But the church to which I belong seems captured by the identification of God and country. Red is a color of the Christian tradition. It's Pentecost. White is a color of the Christian tradition. It's Easter. Blue is the liturgical color for the mother who gave birth to Jesus. But for Christians these colors are never sewn together. When they are sewn together into a flag, they threaten to overwhelm – perhaps even replace – their role in reflecting and forming our vision as God's people. That red, white, and blue have now become Christian colors indicates that the church has been taken captive by a very different narrative than the story of Jesus. It seems the churches have a choice – to be pro-government or to be irrelevant.

I do not envy the challenge preachers faced on the Sunday following September 11. Yet surely it is a good thing the church required those ordained to preach the Gospel to stand before their congregations that Sunday. Of course what they said is important, but at least as important is that they had no choice but to proclaim that God is God and we are not.

The challenge for the church, then as now, is to proclaim the Gospel without that proclamation being captured by false idols.

For example, were they preaching to Americans or Christians? The claim that September 11, 2001, forever changed the world is a claim shaped primarily by the narrative of being an American. As Americans we feel violated, vulnerable, fearful. We hate those who have made us recognize our fear. We hate those who have made it impossible for us to trust our neighbors. We hate the loss of security, the loss of comfort that comes from routine. We want normality. I think we are right to want all this, but we must remember that these desires – if we are Christians – must be shaped by our fear of God. And we must remember – if we are Christians – that our experience of stability and security until now has not been shared by fellow Christians around the world, to say nothing of non-Christians.

How can the church be at this time a people of patience who can take the time to step back in the face of terrible events? Of course, since as I noted I am supposed to be "a sectarian fideistic tribalist," I should have an easy answer such as: "Well, it's part of the continuing accommodation of the churches to America."

## The Tonto principle

I often try to explain the work I have done in theology and ethics by telling an old joke about the Lone Ranger and Tonto. It seems that the Lone Ranger and Tonto found themselves surrounded by 20,000 Sioux in South Dakota. The Lone Ranger turned to Tonto and said "This looks like a pretty tough situation, Tonto. What do you think we ought to do?"

Tonto responded, "What do you mean by 'we,' White Man?"

I use this joke to suggest why my work has been an attempt to help Christians reclaim the Christian "we." For example when George Bush senior declared at the beginning of the Gulf War in 1991, "We must oppose naked aggression wherever it occurs," too many Christians automatically assumed they were included in that "we."

My use of this joke, of course, risks not only being out of date (few college students even know who the Lone Ranger was anymore) but also may oversimplify. The joke seems to suggest that we must choose between being Christian or American. But our lives are too entangled with the stories that make us both American and Christian for easy separation.

My life and work has been an attempt to re-establish the Christian belief that whenever we are told that we must respond in a certain way to oppression, wherever it occurs in the world, Christians ask, "What do you mean by 'we,' White Man?"

## Fear of death

The "we" that distinguishes Christians from Americans, moreover, has everything to do with death. Christians are a community shaped by the practice of baptism. Baptism reminds us far worse things can happen to us than dying. The identification of the Christian "we" with the American "we" indicates that the Christian "we" of baptism has been submerged in the American fear of death. The willingness to die of those who flew the planes into the World Trade Center seems incomprehensible to us. It is almost as if the desperation that drove them to these terrible acts is a parody of our unwillingness to die.

> The willingness to die of those who flew the planes into the World Trade Center seems incomprehensible to us.

The terrorist understanding of life mirrors the recent debate about stem cell research. Stem cell research says that any means can be used to keep us from dying. Its flip side is the equally extreme view that any means can be used to kill people. For example, consider that Senator Strom Thurmond (who is allegedly against abortion) thinks that with stem cell research he's going to live to be 168, get married, and have another kid! It's no wonder, given that kind of extremist mentality, that South Carolina is one of the centers for the United States military bases.

Of course we do not recognize how our fear of death for ourselves or other people has everything to do with our being so wealthy.

Our wealth makes us stupid. It allows us to live in the world without learning the pain that our wealth creates in our neighbors. For example, we would not fund stem cell research if we were a country trying to keep people from dying of hunger. We now assume the legitimacy of our government comes from funding stem cell research to keep us from dying rather than from securing justice for the poor.

> Christians can and should have learned through baptism that the worst thing that can happen to us is not death, but dying for the wrong thing.

Part of the space Christians can and should provide at this time is the space given to us as a people who have learned through baptism that the worst thing that can happen to us is not death, but dying for the wrong thing. Christians are told by our Savior we must prepare for death exactly because we refuse to kill in the name of survival.

The university should also be a space for these kinds of questions. The university has traditionally provided the time and space to free us from assumptions that the way the world is, is the way things have to be. In the current national climate of political correctness, however, the university rarely dares open its mouth, let alone its mind. For example, the university could be a place where the "just war" shapes the study of state actions. What would it be for a political science department to teach international relations from a just war perspective? What would that look like in the terms of the world in which we exist? At Duke, we talk a great deal about being a global university. I don't believe it for a moment. We are a university of the United States of America and cannot imagine serving the world in any way other than through doing what is good for the United States of America.

## Embodying a consumer culture

I think the misery of the American public and the world in which we live can be seen nowhere better than in the suggestion (in many ways quite understandable) that we must take up our responsibilities as citizens and respond to the attacks by shopping. A people who cannot think of anything better to do than shop might sound like a people who are not ready to kill anyone. But not being able to think of anything better to do than shop is precisely the problem. A people who know nothing better to do than to shop may turn out to be the most determinative killers, because at last something interesting has dropped in their laps, and they don't know how to think about it. They have never learned to think about it. They have not provided in their churches and the universities the time and space to think about it.

All of this is a reminder that the sermons preached and the lectures given *after* September 11, 2001, are less significant than the ones that *preceded* September 11. For if Christians had no way of discerning how being Christian might involve tension with being American prior to September 11, 2001, you can be sure that they would be unable to say how their Christian response can and must be distinguished from the American response after that date.

I have tried to think how Augustine might have responded to September 11, 2001. After all, he wrote *The City of God* at least in part to make clear that it was not Christianity that made Rome vulnerable to the barbarians. According to Augustine, Rome was only reaping what Roman pride had sown. Augustine asks us to consider the somewhat surprising fact that something in humility exalts the mind and something in exaltation abases the mind.

> But devout humility makes the mind subject to what is superior. Nothing is superior to God; and that is why humility exalts the mind by making it subject to God. Exaltation, in contrast, derives from a fault in character, and spurns subjection for that reason. Hence it falls away from him who has no superior, and falls lower in consequence. That is why humility is highly prized in the City of God and especially enjoined on the City of God during the time of its pilgrimage in this world; and it receives particular

emphasis in the character of Christ, the king of the City. We are taught by the sacred Scriptures that the fault of exaltation, the contrary of humility, exercises supreme dominion in Christ's adversary, the Devil. This is assuredly the great difference that sunders the two cities of which we are speaking: the one the community of devout men, the other a company of the irreligious… In one city love of God has been given first place, in the other, love of self. (*The City of God*, Book 14, Chapter 13)

## Possessed by ungodly powers

Ask yourself when you last preached or heard a sermon that suggested that most of our lives are determined by pride? When was the last time you preached or heard a sermon that named how we are possessed because of our pride by the powers that take the form of institutions we assume we "control"? When was the last time you heard or preached a sermon that intimated that the pride in "Proud To Be An American" might not be a "good thing," given what Christians think about pride?

Jerry Falwell was, of course, wrong to suggest that what happened was a judgment on American divorce and abortion cultures. He was not only wrong, but the god he assumed was doing the judgment is not the Christian God. After all, God does not punish us for our sins, but our sins are their own punishment. Yet I cannot help but think that Augustine might well have seen in those proud buildings a manifestation of a pride that knows not the humility of Christ.

Let me be clear. I am not suggesting that the people who died on September 11, 2001, "deserved" their deaths. Nor am I suggesting that we should see in that horrible destruction the direct hand of God. Rather I am simply pointing out that as Christians we have been lazy in our thinking and our teaching to the extent we have failed to help one another name how our lives are caught in modes of life Augustine identified with the City of Man. We have allowed God to be relegated to the realm of the "personal." As a result we have no way to narrate America in the way Augustine narrated Rome.

## Reaffirming prior judgments

It is hard not to respond to September 11, 2001, without using the event to confirm one's prior judgments about what is wrong or right about America or, more globally, with "the world." I continue to worry that those who have criticized the war against terrorism, and I count myself among them, have engaged in responses meant to confirm our views held prior to September 11, 2001, about what is wrong with America. Criticism or praise of American foreign policy that provides a context to help us understand "what happened" can be helpful.

~

**If we are to seek truth after September 11, 2001, we must not try to say too much. We must not pretend we have an answer.**

~

I think there is much wrong with America. I think there is and continues to be much wrong with American foreign policy. Yet I must be careful to theologically discipline my outrage.

Which brings me back to silence. Silence inhabits the edges of our words. If we are to seek truth after September 11, 2001, we must not try to say too much. We must not pretend we have an answer to explain what happened or to know what response we – and who is the "we"? – might make.

I have no pacifist foreign policy. I believe the church is God's foreign policy. In the Houston *Catholic Worker* (November 16, 2001) I read an article by Jean Vanier, a man who believes God has saved us from violence by giving us the good work of living with those called "retarded."

Our lives continue to be haunted by the specter of September 11, 2001. Yet life must go on, and we go on keeping on. Is this what Barth meant in 1933 when he said we must go on "as though nothing had happened"? To go on as though nothing has happened can sound like a counsel of despair, of helplessness, of hopelessness. We want to act, to do something to reclaim the way things were. One of the reasons we are so shocked, so violated, by September 11 is that it challenges our prideful presumption that we are in control, that we are going to get out of life alive. To go on "as though nothing had happened" requires us to acknowledge that God is God and we are not.

It is hard to remember that Jesus did not come to make us safe, but rather to make us disciples, citizens of God's new age, a kingdom of surprise. God invites us to respond to September 11 with "small acts of beauty and tenderness," which Jean Vanier tells us, if done with humility and confidence, "will bring unity to the world and break the chain of violence."

# The wrong apocalypse

## Walter Wink

For those trapped in the twin towers of the World Trade Center or in the Pentagon, that fiery hell must have seemed apocalyptic. In the fleeting moments before they leaped from windows or were crushed under melting I-beams, what passed through their minds?

Certainly for those who watched in horror, on the streets or on television in their homes and offices, it must have looked as if a mini end-of-the-world Apocalypse had descended.

Or did it?

In some respects, yes, it was an apocalypse. The word "apocalypse" means "unveiling" – specifically, the unveiling of things to come. What was unveiled for us on September 11 was the prospect of endless acts of terrorism perpetrated by invisible enemies against mostly innocent civilians. In such an apocalyptic moment, as it is generally conceived, the future seems to be closed, inevitable, and inescapable. Since this future cannot be averted, apocalyptic can only call people to personal repentance, so that after the catastrophe they might survive to enjoy either heaven or a transfigured earth.

Eschatology, by contrast, regards the future as open, undetermined, and capable of being changed – if people alter their behavior in time. The urgency of the great prophets of the Old Testament came from their conviction that catastrophe need not happen, that even a small deviation from the current course towards doom might avert it.

Eschatology is concerned about the goal of humanity and the world. Apocalyptic is consumed with the end of the planet earth as it is presently constituted. Prophetic eschatology is ruthlessly realistic, yet incurably hopeful. Apocalyptic has abandoned hope, and looks for miraculous divine intervention.

Apocalyptic has a foreshortened sense of time. It anticipates a final war between the powers of good and evil. By appealing to these absolutes, President Bush has attempted to endow his cause with a kind of ultimacy, in which "those who are not for us are against us." There is no time left; every nation must choose sides.

## The other side of the story

If that were the whole story about apocalyptic, many of us would want nothing to do with it. That is not the whole story, however. There is a positive role for apocalyptic as well as its better known negative. The positive power of apocalyptic lies in its capacity to force humanity to face threats of unimaginable proportions in order to galvanize efforts at self- and social transcendence. Only such Herculean responses can actually rescue people from the threat and make possible the continuation of humanity on the other side.

> The positive power of apocalyptic lies in its capacity to force humanity to face threats of unimaginable proportions in order to galvanize efforts at self- and social transcendence.

Paradoxically, the apocalyptic warning is intended to remove the apocalyptic threat by acts of apocalyptic transcendence.

As the philosopher Gunter Anders put it, we move into the apocalyptic mode when we no longer find ourselves asking, "How shall we live?" and ask instead, "Will we live?" The normal eschatological situation – which gives life urgency by facing us with the inevitability of our own death, the hunger for meaning, and the fear of suffering and loss – becomes apocalyptic when it appears that there is no longer time for normal urgency. Time collapses. The Time of the End becomes the End of Time. Those who are "not yet non-existing" must do everything in their power to make the End Time endless. "Since we believe in the possibility of the 'End of Time,' we are Apocalyptics," Anders wrote in the middle of the nuclear terror of 1962, "but since we fight against this man-made Apocalypse, we are – and this has never existed before – 'Anti-Apocalyptics.'"

The apocalyptic situation dwarfs our human capacity and reduces us to powerlessness. The negative response is passivity and despair; the positive is a superhuman effort and assault on the impossible. The negative version of apocalyptic leaves us feeling that we are smaller than ourselves, incapable of the required response. Positive apocalyptic, by contract, calls on our every power to avert what seems inevitable. "Nothing can save us that is possible," the poet W.H. Auden intoned over the madness of the nuclear crisis; "We who must die demand a miracle." And the miracle we got came about because people like the physician Helen Caldicott refused to accept nuclear annihilation. But she did it by forcing her hearers to visualize the consequences of their inaction.

## The tools for fighting despair

Imagination, says Anders, is the sole organ capable of conveying a truth so overwhelming that we cannot take it in. Hence the bizarre imagery that always accompanies apocalyptic. Optimists want to believe that reason will save us. They want to prevent us from becoming really afraid. The anti-apocalyptist, on the contrary, insists that it is our capacity to fear that is too small and that does not correspond to the magnitude of the present danger. Therefore, says Anders, the anti-apocalyptist attempts to increase our capacity to fear: "Don't fear fear; have the courage to be frightened, and to frighten others too. Frighten thy neighbor as thyself."

> ∽
> It is our capacity to fear that is too small and that does not correspond to the magnitude of the present danger.
> ∽

This is no ordinary fear, however; it is a fearless fear, since it dares at last to face the real magnitude of the danger. And it is a loving fear, since it embraces fear in order to save the generations to come. That is why everything the anti-apocalyptist says is said in order *not* to become true.

If we do not stubbornly keep in mind how probable the disaster is, and if we do not act accordingly, we will not be able to prevent the warnings from coming true. There is nothing more frightening than to be right. And if some, paralyzed by the gloomy likelihood of the catastrophe, should already have lost their courage, they too still have the chance to prove their love of humanity by heeding the cynical maxim: "Let's go on working as though we had the right to hope. Our despair is none of their business."

## Anti-apocalyptic before their time

Anders' insight is fundamental, because it suggests that some of the biblical apocalyptics were really anti-apocalyptics. They said what they said in order that it not become true. Jonah understood this, and for that reason fled his task. He knew God was sending him to preach doom so that it would not happen, thus making him a liar.

A positive outcome might be conceivable, if the human race rises to its capacities and meets the future faithfully. But if it does not, then the apocalyptic nightmare may indeed descend on us. Luke warns,

> Be on guard so that your hearts are not weighed down with dissipation and drunkenness and the worries of this life, and that day catch you unexpectedly like a trap. For it will come on all who live on the face of the whole earth. Be alert at all times, praying that you may have the strength to escape all these things that will take place, and to stand before the Son of Man. (Luke 21:34-36)

It is not difficult to see in that warning the perils that threaten the very viability of life on earth today. Global warming, the ozone hole, overpopulation, starvation and malnutrition, war, unemployment, the destruction of species and of the rain forests, pollution of water and air, pesticide and herbicide poisoning, errors in genetic engineering, erosion of topsoil, overfishing, anarchy and crime, the possibility of nuclear mishap, chemical warfare, or all-out nuclear war – together, or in some cases singly, these dangers threaten to "catch us unexpectedly, like a trap." Our inability thus far to measure ourselves against these threats is an ominous portent that apocalypse has already rendered us powerless.

### Putting apocalypse in perspective

Terrible as it was, the destruction of the World Trade Center was not an apocalypse. That horror will slowly recede. Other acts of infamy may take place. But we can anticipate a time when terrorism will decline. Nor are we helpless. We have the means to stop at least many, perhaps even most, of the terrorist attacks that may be hurled against us. But we can see the other side of this catastrophe, when life will feel normal again.

The threats to our very survival that I listed above, however, will not go away. They could well spell the end of humanity, and even of most sentient life. This is the awful truth that we have yet to recognize. We are living in an apocalyptic time disguised as normal, and that is why we have not responded appropriately. If we are in the midst of the sixth great extinction, as scientists tell us we are, our response has in no way been commensurate with the danger. We *homo sapiens* are witnessing the greatest annihilation of species in the last 65 million years, and our children may live to witness ecocide with their own eyes. So while we are understandably preoccupied with terrorism, and must do everything necessary to stamp it out, we must at the same time wake up to these more serious threats that could effectively end life on this planet.

But the verdict is not yet in. It is late, but a positive response to the apocalypse of our times is still possible. Consider South Africa. When I was there in the 1980s, it appeared that armed revolution was inevitable.

Our inability thus far to measure ourselves against these threats is an ominous portent that apocalypse has already rendered us powerless.

We are living in an apocalyptic time disguised as normal, and that is why we have not responded appropriately.

Blacks were becoming more desperate by the day. Teenage boys were confronting the police and army without concern for their safety. Chaos was beginning to overtake the townships, as children, outraged by the timorousness of their parents, seized the initiative themselves. Whites were taking an increasingly hard line. It was a recipe for disaster. The whole scene reeked of an apocalypse of the negative sort.

Then the most unexpected thing happened. The white government chose, under intense internal and international pressure, to relinquish power. It negotiated with its former black enemies a process that led to the election of a black president, a model constitution, and relatively low casualties, considering the alternatives.

No one, to my knowledge, anticipated this turn of events. What had appeared as an inevitable (negative) apocalyptic bloodbath turned out to have been a (positive) apocalyptic situation instead, thanks to the "anti-apocalyptists" who rose to the occasion.

## Choosing between alternatives

Rather than two opposed scenarios, then, negative and positive apocalyptic seem to represent two alternatives. If the current evil course is adhered to, despite the warnings of the prophets (and South Africa was blessed with an abundance of these), the outcome will be negative apocalypse. But if the warnings of the anti-apocalyptists are heeded, the outcome can be a miracle (see, for example, Jeremiah 18:7-11). Perhaps, then, we might read Revelation 18-20 as the dire negative apocalyptic prospect for those societies that refuse to do justice, and Revelation 21-22 as the propitious positive apocalyptic prospect for those societies that repent and do what is right.

Eschatology is a line stretching out to the distant, possibly infinite, future. That is the horizon of hope, possibility, and becoming. Apocalyptic, on the other hand, is a detour, caused by an immediate crisis threatening whole societies. Negative apocalyptic paralyzes us into inaction; positive apocalyptic challenges us to transcend ourselves, opening to the unexpected possibilities thrust upon us. Usually, when the crisis passes, normal eschatology is reinstated. But in our day, the apocalyptic crisis may not pass.

Walter Wink's latest book is *The Human Being: Jesus and the Enigma of the Son of Man,* Published by Fortress Press, from which this essay is adapted. Copyright 2001 Christian Century Foundation. Reproduced by permission from the October 17, 2001 issue of *Christian Century.* Subscriptions $49/yr from P.O. Box 378, Mt. Morris, IL, 61054. 1-800-208-4097

# 4

# Rethinking evil

## James Taylor

In the weeks and months that followed September 11, the concept of evil made a remarkable comeback.

For most of my life, evil was not a term commonly used. In mainline church circles, people avoided the word. Sermons spoke of human weakness or moral failing. The social sciences called it psychosis, disorder, or dysfunction. We banished evil from our vocabularies. Flip Wilson routinely got laughs by announcing, "The devil made me do it."

But since September 11, "evil" has made a bigger comeback than the U.S. defense budget.

U.S. president George W. Bush referred to "evil-doers" in almost every public appearance. Defense Secretary Donald Rumsfeld and other officials echoed the description. Even Canadian prime minister Jean Chretien and British prime minister Tony Blair jumped on the bandwagon.

Nor was this usage a mere flash in the pan. Five months later, in his State of the Union address, Bush firmly cemented evil back into the American psyche by naming an "axis of evil" – Iraq, Iran, and North Korea.

## Misunderstood terms

"Evil" has suddenly become a convenient label for anyone and anything we consider morally reprehensible. But I suspect that most of those using the term have neither studied the meaning of the term, nor considered its implications.

One writer (I wish I had noted his name) cleverly noted that "evil" is "live" spelled backward. From that, he deduced that evil is intrinsically anti-life, and therefore pro-death. It's a clever play on words, but it works only in English.

It reminds me of an evangelist who went to Japan. "I have come here to preach the gospel," he began. His translator duly translated the sentence into Japanese. The evangelist continued, "And you can all see that 'gospel' begins with the word 'go'!"

The translator fell silent, because the word play applied only in English. In Japanese, gospel and go had no connection.

Karl Menninger, 30 years ago, wrote a little book called *Whatever Happened to Sin?* His thesis was that we had sanitized sin – and along with it, the notion of evil. Sin and evil are shadow images of each other.

Menninger wasn't suggesting that we didn't sin anymore. Rather, he argued, we had found new ways of describing sin that didn't make it *sound* like sin anymore.

Menninger suggested three ways that we avoid dealing with the reality of sin:

## 1. Turning sin into illness

We treat sin as an illness. It may be psychological, or physical, or chemical. Whatever the cause, the illness controls the behavior, not the person. Therefore the illness is to blame, not the person.

Treating sin as illness offers hope. Illnesses are curable – or at least treatable. Even terminal illnesses like cancer or cystic fibrosis can have their effects eased. As a result, there is not as much social stigma attached to an illness as to a sin. (AIDS still has a stigma attached to it, as leprosy did in ancient times. But as we learn more about AIDS, and realize how many people contracted it through no fault of their own – through blood transfusions, for example – even that stigma is fading.)

But blaming the illness removes responsibility from the person who harms others. Significantly, President Bush did not offer excuses for Osama bin Laden, by suggesting he suffered from paranoia or megalomania. He said bin Laden was evil. Period.

## 2. Turning sin into crime

Second, said Menninger, we make sin a crime. This shifts responsibility from the moral to the legal sphere.

> "What had been the business of priests," Menninger wrote, "becomes the business of the police, assisted by lawyers and judges and jailers. Between them, they seek and seize, detain, hold, humble, hurt, deport, execute, or discharge their 'sinners,' now called criminals." (p. 110)

This shift is not, in itself, a bad thing. If I were accused of a crime – rightly or wrongly – I would certainly rather trust even a corrupt justice system than an angry mob.

But this transformation of sin also has a negative effect. Where sin as disease removes responsibility from the sinner, sin as crime removes responsibility from citizens. We no longer need to strive for harmonious relationships in our neighborhood; we call the police. We no longer need to support abused families; we call in the social workers. Like Pontius Pilate, the redefinition allows us to wash our hands of the evil going on around us.

It also enables us to deny that any wrongdoing has happened. If it was legal, it couldn't be wrong. I hear this argument so often, I'm amazed that those who make it don't realize their underlying assumption. A company's toxic wastes poison a whole town's wells, or irreparably damage children's nervous systems. But the companies disavow responsibility. They acted within government guidelines, they insist. So they can't have done anything wrong.

Surprisingly, both Osama bin Laden and George Bush used this defense for their actions. Bin Laden cited the Qur'an, the only legal code he accepts, as legal justification for an attack on America; Bush defined the search for bin Laden as a police action.

### 3. Blaming sin on society

Third, we treat sin as the product of a dysfunctional society. The group or the "system" is responsible, not the individual. People didn't commit crimes because they were bad, but because they had been abused as children, or brought up in the wrong neighborhood, or adversely affected by drugs or smoking or alcohol during pregnancy. They didn't sin; they were innocent victims of circumstances beyond their control.

The notion of collective responsibility, particularly, removes any blame from the individual. As comedian Anna Russell cracked, in one of her skits, "Everything I do that's wrong is someone else's fault!"

## Collective absolution

But there's an implicit assumption involved here, that sins are only done by individuals. If no one person did wrong, goes the assumption, then whatever it was can't have been wrong. By this presumption, evil, to be evil, must be attributable to a single person.

> By this presumption, evil, to be evil, must be attributable to a single person.

That tactic certainly applied following the September 11 tragedy. Within days, America as a whole had found its villain – Osama bin Laden.

The entire American campaign against terrorism became focused on capturing, and punishing, one man. *Time* magazine almost made him their Newsmaker of the Year. His picture adorned magazine covers and newspaper front pages; his video clips appeared on more television screens around the world than reruns of M\*A\*S\*H.

That assumption had two immediate effects.

First, it turned every other conspirator into a mere robot. It treated bin Laden as the only brains behind the conspiracy to hijack four airliners and to use them as flying bombs. As if he and he alone pulled the strings that got his puppets through security, into the cockpits, taking over the controls, aiming the planes at their targets.

Second, it granted absolution to Americans. They could brush aside that question that had initially tormented them: "Why do they hate us so much?" Now they could simply ask, "Why does *he* hate us so much?" Osama bin Laden became the aberration, the odd man out, the exception that proves the rule. The American way of life emerged unscathed.

Significantly, President Bush's "axis of evil" speech failed to generate a similar public response. He simply did not understand that in the common perception, evil needs to be lodged in a single individual. Treating an entire system as an enemy, as Menninger pointed out, leaves no one to blame.

## Not the opposite of good

Most of those who used the term "evil" to describe bin Laden and his Al-Qaeda network – including, I'm sure, President Bush and his advisors – probably assumed that evil is the opposite of good. It's not.

It's a comfortable way of thinking. Because if your enemies are evil, then you must, almost by definition, be good. And the more virulently you oppose those enemies, the "gooder" you must become.

> Most of those who used the term "evil" assumed that evil is the opposite of good.

Unfortunately, it doesn't work that way.

That dualistic perspective was rejected by theologians and philosophers long ago. In the Christian tradition, Manichaeism ran rampant in the first millennium. It spread from Spain all the way to China. It influenced many of the early Christian thinkers, including St. Augustine of Hippo, before being denounced as a heresy.

But Manichaeism was merely a Christian version of Zoroastrianism, an ancient Persian religion. It still survives among the Parsees of India.

Zoroastrianism sees the world as a battleground between two gods: a good one, most often called Ahura Mazda, and an evil one, Ahriman.

But experience should tell us that, far from being the opposite of good, evil usually grows out of something good.

Remember the story of the Garden of Eden? Everything in that Garden was created by God. And the Bible assures us that "it was good." God created the humans who disobeyed, the fruit that they coveted, the serpent who incited them to taste it.

Biblically, therefore, original evil can only have come out of good.

The problem, in Eden, was not the knowledge of good and evil. All would not be well in the world if we were all utterly oblivious to any concept of good or evil. Indeed, the entire thrust of the Bible – from the Hebrew prophets through Jesus Christ to the mission outreach of the early Christian church – was the preference of good over evil. Consider Paul's lists of virtues:

> Whatever is true, whatever is honorable, whatever is just, whatever is pure, whatever is pleasing, whatever is commendable, if there is any excellence and if there is anything worthy of praise… (Philippians 4:8)

The evil in Eden was the desire, in the serpent's words, to "be like God." To take knowledge of good and evil, in other words, to an extreme.

Thus good, taken to an extreme, can become evil.

## How evil becomes evil

In past centuries, questions of good and evil were usually worked out from axiomatic principles. Today, we have other tools.

Some views, as I indicated above, recognize that people do not necessarily intend to do evil – rather, they find themselves caught by forces over which they have no control. They may have contributed to behavior that can now be classed as evil, perhaps by taking social drinking to an excess, perhaps by having certain violent motivations.

But at a certain point, the malady took over. It now runs them, instead of the other way around.

Today, we have other means of evaluating good and evil. And one of the most interesting comes from communications theory.

It's not a bad place to start. Because, as should be obvious all along, evil cannot exist independently. No one is intrinsically evil (even if we have mythologized a wholly evil creature called Satan). Only as one person's behavior has certain effects on others do we characterize that person, or that person's actions, as evil.

## How good becomes evil

Simply put, evil occurs only in relationships. That implies communication. That makes communications theory a valid means of determining what is, and what is not, evil.

Shortly before his death, Marshall McLuhan and his son Eric McLuhan began developing what they called the "Laws of Media." Both had been stung by criticisms

> Simply put, evil occurs only in relationships.

that they were dilettantes, dabbling in communications theory without any underlying principles to guide them. So they began exploring those principles.

They found that "media" covered much more than they had previously imagined. "Media" included not just radio and television and newspapers – it encompassed every form of human communication, including arts and crafts, manufactured products, and even social institutions. All of these, they concluded, are ways in which we communicate with each other.

Because communication is a process, not an object, these laws predict processes, not products. They're not like the laws of chemistry, for example. In chemistry, if you mix, say, pure hydrogen and pure oxygen, and introduce a spark or a flame, you will get an explosion that produces water. If you mix hydrochloric acid and lye, you'll get a vigorous reaction that produces ordinary table salt.

Things don't work that way with communications theory. If you mix a new element (such as printing) with an old culture (such as Europe in the 1500s) you won't get asparagus or cuckoo clocks. Rather, you get a new way of thinking, which today we define as literacy. You get a rejection of old patterns of faith, which we call The Reformation. And you create, strangely enough, a new and previously unknown disability that we call illiteracy.

The McLuhans argued that every new communications technology fulfilled four – and only four – functions.

- It enhanced something that already existed.
- It made something that already existed obsolete.
- It retrieved some technology from the past.
- And finally, when pushed to an extreme, it "flipped" into the opposite of what was intended.

Of these four, only the last concerns us. Because, as I said earlier, the McLuhans found that these "Laws of Media" applied not merely to communications, but to all human creations.

Consider some examples. The freeway was designed to speed up traffic. But when pushed past its carrying capacity, it turns into a parking lot.

The Internet was intended to disseminate information quickly. But when a website gets overloaded, it crashes. Nothing gets out.

Motherhood is presumed to be a universal good. But mothering, overdone, becomes stifling.

The pattern is clear. But significantly, it applies only to human creations. A lily of the field, taken to an extreme, will not flip into anything else. A lily just is. A cloud will never be anything but a cloud. Nor will a tree. Or an ocean.

But any human construction, pushed to its limits, will flip into its opposite. Accurate spelling and grammar enhance communication, but turned into an obsession, they become pedantry that impedes communication. Too many social drinks turn into anti-social alcoholism. Our toys become tyrants. Our possessions possess us.

## The trap of good intentions

This pattern explains why good intentions can so often go sour. We believe that because a project started out with good intentions, it must necessarily be good at all times.

That is why the vast majority of Americans could not see anything wrong in bombing Afghanistan into submission. Or arresting and jailing people merely on suspicion of involvement in terrorism. Or imposing American-designed security measures on countries that have never had a plane hijacking, and that are so far away that no plane hijacked there could possibly fly to the United States without refueling.

> ∼
> **We believe that because a project started out with good intentions, it must necessarily be good at all times.**
> ∼

Because if terrorism is wrong, anything that combats terrorism must be right, mustn't it?

No. It may be just as wrong, just as dangerous.

During the First World War, British commanders wanted to protect their pilots from enemy fire. So they began armoring their planes. Fragile flying machines that had trouble staying aloft at any time got loaded down with armor; they became lumbering airborne tanks, as maneuverable and safe as a flying brick. Allied airborne casualties increased, instead of decreasing. It wasn't until some pilots flagrantly disregarded orders and lightened their planes by dumping armor that British air forces once again became competitive.

In the same way, programs to provide housing for transients in urban cores can encourage more transients. Welfare payments intended to relieve suffering can make recipients captives. Drugs intended to relieve pain can become addictive.

Any good intention taken to an extreme will "flip" – to use the McLuhans' term – into evil.

## Crossing invisible lines

But the term "flip" is deceiving. Because there is no single point at which the reversal occurs. "Dissolves" might be a more accurate metaphor.

During the Depression years before World War II, King Gordon taught theology at United Theological College, on the campus of McGill University in Montreal.

King Gordon was a founder of Canada's socialist political party, the Cooperative Commonwealth Federation or CCF, which later became today's New Democratic Party. His theology reflected his socialist views. Eventually, his books and his radical views made him unwelcome at United College. This was, after all, a time which still tended to identify sin with playing cards or drinking rum. Gordon moved on to New York, where he became managing editor of *The Nation*. Later, he served the United Nations in Korea, the Middle East, and the Congo, before finishing his career teaching international relations at universities in Alberta and in Ottawa.

> Evil is never something we choose to do. It's something we find ourselves trapped in.

Sixty years later, we're just beginning to catch up to King Gordon's insights. Basically, he said that *evil is never something we choose to do. It's something we find ourselves trapped in.* It's not something we're tempted *into*, but something we're *already in.*

That makes perfect sense, if we consider the alternative – love. Very few people deliberately set out to fall in love. Rather, they discover – often to their distinct surprise – that they have fallen in love with a person they used to think of only as a colleague, a friend, even just a date. Why should we assume that evil works any differently? Thus Gordon argued that sinners or evil-doers realize with a shock, some day, that past actions, even well-intentioned past actions, have snared them in a sticky web.

Evil is like Wiley Coyote chasing the Road Runner. Wiley is halfway across the canyon, feet flailing, before he realizes he has no ground under him anymore.

You only discover you're in quicksand when you start sinking. When swimming, you only realize you're in over your head when you try to touch bottom – and can't. That's the nature of sin, said Gordon. Real sin. Not the trivial little personal faults like missing church one Sunday or sneaking a smoke behind the barn. But systemic sin, the kind of sin that floods a whole society and carries us along with it.

Gordon's context was the labor struggles of the 1920s and 1930s, when company owners and industrialists used all kinds of what we would now call "dirty tricks" to prevent labor unions from organizing. Gordon clearly took the unions' side. But he did not assume that the owners and employers were necessarily evil. A lumber baron in New Brunswick, Gordon wrote, does not attempt to bust unions because he thinks it is wrong. Rather, he does so because he thinks it is *right*. He sees unions as a threat, a danger. They upset the historic order. They are taking away from him something he considers his, by right of ownership. So he fights against them, with all his might.

> That's what makes both yesterday's lumber baron and today's terrorist so dangerous – they think they are *right*.

That's what makes both yesterday's lumber baron and today's terrorist so dangerous – they think they are *right*.

If the lumber baron really thought he was wrong, suggested Gordon, it would be possible to reason with him. It would be possible to show him other alternatives, which might serve both him and the union better. But because he is convinced that he is right, he can change only when he finds himself suddenly "convicted," brought to a different awareness of his actions.

## Like a conversion experience

The recognition of being trapped in sin comes like a conversion experience.

The lumber baron, ruthlessly battling the unions with every tool available, thought all the time that he was doing what was best for the industry. And then something – perhaps a personal contact with someone harmed by his policies – opens his eyes. He's shattered.

A white resident of the southern states doesn't think she's prejudiced. Indeed, she thinks she's unusually considerate of black people. Suddenly, she realizes how even her kindnesses perpetuate a historical injustice. She's devastated.

Gordon argued that people never intend to commit sin – rather they suddenly discover themselves trapped in it. Something opens their eyes, and they see that what they had thought was right turned out to be wrong.

Now, this concept should be immediately acceptable to evangelicals, because it is the basis of conversion. One discovers oneself to be a sinner. One did not set out to be a sinner.

> ∼
> **The discovery that one is implicit in sin and evil always comes as a shock.**
> ∼

It also makes sense to liberals, because it acknowledges that sin is a social situation. One does what seems to be right in society's eyes – and later discovers that society was wrong. So William Wilberforce realized that slavery was wrong. So did Abraham Lincoln, even though several of his predecessors as president themselves had had slaves.

The discovery that one is implicit in sin and evil always comes as a shock. It comes as an awareness that one has somehow stepped over an invisible line that one had not been aware was there at all.

## Shades of gray

This kind of discovery comes only in hindsight. Good and evil are not divided like black and white. Rather, they are shades of gray. Moving along a path of gray that shades progressively from dark to light, no one but a graphics designer could hope to define the exact point at which the percentage of white surpasses the percentage of black. Some would guess too soon; some, too late. But as they continue along the continuum, everyone will discover that they have passed the point of equality.

But there is another discovery needed. And that is that simply going the opposite direction is no solution.

Slavery was bad. Merely casting slaves loose did not improve their lot. They had been cared for – they still needed to be cared for.

> ～
> **Simply going the opposite direction is no solution.**
> ～

Choose any virtue you value. Imagine what would happen if it became obsessive. Would it still be as lovable? As admirable?

Take thrift to an extreme, and it turns into stinginess or greed. Scrooge probably started with good intentions, just like most of the businesses that downsized their most loyal staffs into the streets to improve short-term profit margins during the 1990s.

Neatness can become a fetish. Personal hygiene, overdone, turns into squeamishness about getting dirty, about getting involved in anything that brings one close to the "unwashed masses." Unchecked cooperativeness can make you a doormat to be exploited by anyone. Strength of will can lead to tyranny; independence to machismo; friendliness to intrusion.

Yes, even love. Parental love, overdone, turns into overprotectiveness, spoiling, dominance, the often-satirized "Jewish Mama" stereotype, the need to control one's children even when they have grown up... In the same way, intimacy can easily transform into possessiveness, jealously, lust...

> ～
> **A virtue becomes evil when it becomes an obsession, when it is taken to an extreme.**
> ～

A virtue, in other words, is never absolute. It exists in relationship, in balance, with other virtues and values. It becomes evil only when it becomes an obsession, when it is taken to an extreme.

## Too much or too little

Greek philosopher Aristotle understood that, 23 centuries ago. He talked about moderation in everything. British author Lyall Watson commented that, for Aristotle, desires "become bad, and may be identified as wrong desires, if we want too much." And he continues:

> But – and this I think is Aristotle's most vital contribution
> to the discussion of evil, contradicting the schools of hair-
> shirt discipline which turn abstinence into a virtue – such
> desires may be bad and wrong also if we want *too little*.
>
> Aristotelian ethics is the ethics of "just enough" ...
> Enough is enough, even of a good thing. Even moral virtues
> such as courage are good only if they lie along the narrow
> mean. A man who fears everything becomes a coward, but
> a man who fears nothing is a dangerous fool. (*Dark Nature*,
> pp. 7-8)

The limits to which one pushes virtue to turn it into evil, then, can go *either* way – either too much *or* too little. Too much and too little are equally dangerous.

~
**Too much and too little are equally dangerous.**
~

For examples, consider the chemicals in our diets. Too much selenium and too little are alike harmful to our bodies.

Too much iodine is poisonous. That's what made it an effective disinfectant. But when I was a child, all salt was iodized. Because too little iodine led to goiters and thyroid problems.

Both hypoglycemia and hyperglycemia are hazardous.

The principle applies even to our most common elements. Too little water, you die of thirst. Too much, you drown. Too little oxygen, you asphyxiate; too much, your cells oxidize themselves to death. Too little fire, we freeze; too much, we burn.

In schools, there has been much fuss about child abuse, sexual or physical. Many Canadian school boards have ruled that there must be no physical contact of any kind between teachers and pupils. But that's not much improvement. Because the opposite of child abuse (too much physical contact) is child neglect (too little contact).

If these examples seem trivial, consider the corollary: *"The greater and better the virtue, the more terrible it's going to be if it goes wrong."* Those are not my words. I wish they were, but they came from Lady Helen Oppenheimer, writer and moral philosopher, on the CBC program *Ideas*. She went on: "It is the glorious qualities of human beings which are (most) corruptible…"

An old Latin maxim encapsulated this wisdom. *Corruptio optimi pessima*. That is, "When the best is corrupted, it becomes the worst."

The good, therefore, always lies somewhere between two extremes.

## Oscillating between extremes

In New York and Washington, on September 11, we saw one extreme. A group of fanatics committed suicide for a cause.

It's questionable whether the response was, or was not, another extreme. Certainly some of the reactions were extremes. University professors were censured, disciplined, investigated, and reputedly in a few cases fired, for asking questions about the nature and scope of the responses. Freedom of speech and movement were restricted. Paranoia reigned.

Coming through Los Angeles airport, on an international flight five months later, my wife and I stood in line for almost two hours, inching forward through serpentine barriers. In all that time, we were under observation. No outside person had any contact with us. We could not alter anything in our passports or baggage. Yet we had our passports checked five times, as if we could or would change our identity while still in the lineup. Our hand luggage was scanned three times, our checked baggage X-rayed twice, as if we could have added anything to it while isolated from any outside contact.

> The U.S. reaction to terrorism revealed more paranoia than efficiency, more fear than vision.

I have no objection to airport security. But one thorough check – I offer the International Airport at Belfast, in Northern Ireland, as an example – would accomplish far more than five perfunctory checks done by bored employees with glazed eyes.

The U.S. reaction to terrorism revealed more paranoia than efficiency, more fear than vision.

Nathan Baxter, dean of Washington National Cathedral, has said,

> We must remember that evil does not wear a turban, a tunic,
> a yarmulke, or a cross. Evil wears the garment of a human
> heart woven from the threads of hate and fear.

Tragically, I'm afraid, we have learned little from the fallout from September 11. "They" are still evil; "we" are still right.

And so there will be another tragedy. And another.

A little well-thought-through theology could make a great deal of difference in our response to evil.

# 5

# Flaws in our systems of governance

## Senator Lois Wilson

The terrorist attack of September 11 set off shock waves of disbelief and anger, and evoked apocalyptic language about good against evil. The world has known terrorist attacks before, but nothing to match the large scale of this one, nor the audacity, nor the magnitude of the response worldwide. Terrorist activity has been around for centuries, but now it is not spears, arrows, or guns. It is knives, fully fueled airplanes, and in the future it could be nerve gas, anthrax, smallpox, or nuclear weapons.

Because the event was unprecedented for many of us, we became aware of the inadequacy of the usual analytic tools or categories that enable us to make sense of what is happening. There are very different perceptions of its meaning, depending partly on where you live in the world, whether you are part of mainstream or marginalized culture of your country, and whether you are part of the machinery of political power or not.

It will take some time to clarify an ambiguous situation, which the media by and large has oversimplified. Indeed, in the Canadian media six months later, there had been no serious sustained analysis of American foreign policy vis-à-vis the Middle East in relation to the attacks, but only endless 24-hour coverage of troops in Afghanistan. Much of the media coverage reminded me sharply of what happened during World War II when both sides misused religion and claimed a mission from God against the opposing side.

Is the threat of terrorism best met by massive armed force? The recent experience of Israel suggests that it is not. Certainly, killing women and children in Afghan villages does not seem to me to be an appropriate Canadian response.

## Redefining terrorism

The word most frequently used about September 11 was "terrorism," although there has been little attempt at a serious definition of what is meant by this term. Indeed, when Canada brought down its legislation to address the situation, the term was so broadly defined that Nelson Mandela would have fit the definition. Ironically, he was made an "honorary citizen of Canada" at just about the same time as the government was passing the legislation.

> I myself would have been defined as a terrorist.

I myself would have been defined as a terrorist, since I supported Mandela's struggle "for religious, ideological, or political reasons," and canvassed Canadians for money to support his struggle. The anti-apartheid struggle in South Africa had as one of its clearly defined goals to destabilize a regime and confound the existing systems. So I fitted the Canadian definition perfectly. And yet a proposed amendment to Bill C-36, brought by Canadian Civil Liberties Association, was not accepted. Terrorist activity, the amendment proposed, "does not include an act directed against a regime outside of Canada that has a system of government not based on the freely given consent of the governed if such act does not target innocent civilians or serious violence."

The wording of this definition suggests to me that Canadian Christians will need to be more careful about supporting wars of liberation in other countries than we have been in the past.

## Misleading perceptions

One common perception holds that the Western alliance is attacking those who have started a "war against civilization." If that is your perception, then you will support either a retaliatory war or a war of self-defense, using traditional methods in a traditional military response:

bombings, ground troops, sheer might and force. Canada supported this version of the attacks by promising all support to the U.S.A.

A Quaker friend of mine claims that the word "war" does not apply to this situation. We use this metaphor to manage the shock of something strange. By comparing the attacks of September 11 with something familiar, we comfort ourselves that we know how to respond appropriately.

But terrorism is a tactic of violence. It needs a response appropriate to that understanding. It will take consistent intelligence to root out the terrorists and to engage the vast numbers of moderate Arabs and Muslims as committed partners against the violence of terrorism. It will require redefining relationships with the government in regions under attack, and a host of other strategies.

> By comparing the attacks of September 11 with something familiar, we comfort ourselves that we know how to respond.

By contrast, calling this conflict a war makes matters worse. It calls forth a response that is off the mark, like the round-the-clock bombing of Afghanistan. In my view, this is *not* a war. It may be *like* a war, but that overused metaphor leads us into inappropriate responses where even more innocent civilians are killed.

Canada lost an opportunity in Afghanistan. Historically, we have played a role as peacemaker. We could have reclaimed that role, but we didn't.

Nor is this conflict primarily a clash of civilizations. Christians know that no particular civilization has universal validity, and that our hope for the future is not dependent on the victory of our civilization.

Another widely circulated perception is that it was a criminal act, a crime against humanity. This is clearer to deal with, since appropriate responses are established in international law. More support needs to be given to the nascent International Criminal Court – which, incidentally, the U.S.A. does not support for fear of some of its own people being brought before that court.

## How the world has not changed

The initial attacks were highly symbolic. The targets were all symbols of the pride and power of America: the economy (the twin towers of the World Trade Center), the military (the Pentagon), and the aborted attack on political power (the White House).

> This symbolic level of conflict requires a deeper analysis, particularly by the faith communities.

This symbolic level of conflict requires a deeper analysis, particularly by the faith communities. Konrad Raiser of the World Council of Churches has pointed out that all secular power and symbols depend on religious symbols to legitimize them. What insights can religious symbols give us that could enhance global community? That is not a rhetorical question; only churches and faith groups working together can begin to answer it.

A decade after the Cold War ended, the present enormous military build-up risks dividing the world into two camps all over again. What are the implications for humans rights, in Canada and around the world?

The cliché is that September 11 changed the world forever. I think not. Many of us have known that the world has always been subject to betrayal, despair, terrorism, suffering, violence, and death. Indeed, knowledge of that reality is part of the Christian understanding of humankind. An estimated 35,000 children died of malnutrition worldwide on September 11, and continue to do so every day. Does the fact that most of them were not American children lend credence to the cliché of the world being changed forever?

American military actions in Afghanistan need to be understood in historical context. They are another instance of the U.S. policy of projecting its power to render other countries accessible to Western interests. This has been evident in Nicaragua, El Salvador, Chile, Guatemala, Panama, and Kuwait.

Economic turndown was present long before September 11, and will continue. Poverty and the gap between the rich and the poor will continue, until the cesspools of poverty that breed anger and despair are drained. The terrorists are generally young men who see few hopeful options for the future. Rightly or wrongly, their organization offered a ray of hope in societies that have too little hope. We need to alter the idea that the world is against them, and we need to target the deprivations they suffer. An increased budget for Development Aid is desirable, but there also needs to be structural economic change between rich and poor countries and equitable trading arrangements to ensure a level playing field. Otherwise, international conflicts and internal civil wars will continue to claim the lives of thousands.

> **The terrorists are generally young men who see few hopeful options for the future.**

## What has changed

What *has* changed is the increased polarization between the north and the south, and between Christians and Muslims. In spite of the efforts of religious leaders to prevent it, the polarization is being understood as the Western world *vs* Islam – although that is tempered by the fact that interest in learning about Islam is at an all-time high. Yet a planned interfaith service in front of the Ontario legislature had to be cancelled because Jews were afraid of being targeted, and Muslims feared stereotyping.

Interfaith dialogue will have to be approached much more carefully now.

Another significant change is the realization of American vulnerability – both by Americans themselves, and by the rest of the world who thought it was the world's most secure country. Some people hoped that this increased sense of vulnerability by Americans would lead to increasing identification and solidarity with people who are vulnerable in other parts of the world, but the U.S.A. has officially moved in quite a different direction.

Increased security measures for its citizens are an immediate natural response to vulnerability, and many Western countries immediately began to make those changes, primarily through legislation and governance. Almost all countries fell into step with President Bush's coalition of the "good" against the "evil," even though many new measures subverted the democracy we all claimed to be protecting.

Canada also rushed to pass massive security legislation.

In the process, though, the border between Canada and the U.S.A. has become a fault line. The border has been a defining issue for Canadians ever since the American Declaration of Independence, the flood of refugees we call United Empire Loyalists, and the War of 1812.

The U.S. military response to terrorism makes the border a symbolic as well as practical issue. As Pierre Trudeau said, Canada is a mouse living next door to an elephant. Canada is also working towards integration of its immigration, refugee, and border security measures with the U.S.A. Since early 2002, Canada has put its armed forces in Afghanistan under American military control.

But why should we put our forces under the control of a country that consistently refuses to sign on to international law?

## An avalanche of legislation

The magnitude of terrorist-inspired laws in Western democracies – new laws as well as amendments to existing legislation – make it unwieldy to attempt to catalogue those laws in this article. However, by February 2002 the U.S.A. had passed 23 new anti-terrorism laws; announced 20 executive orders, decisions, or declarations; and instituted a variety of new regulations. Michigan, New Jersey, and New York had all prepared new state legislation addressing terrorism. As well there were 14 pages of resolutions, legislation with and without floor action, ranging from designation of Sept 11 as "Patriotic Day" to the "Show Your Pride in the Military" Act of 2001.

India, France, Australia, Japan, the UK, and Pakistan all rushed into place new laws governing real and imagined threats to security. And of course, Israel still has in place its Prevention of Terrorism Ordinance passed in 1948.

Canada's legislative response to the September 11 attacks have had four chief characteristics.

- First, the *speed* at which legislative initiatives were enacted into law.
- Second, the *comprehensive nature* of the anti-terrorist legislation and the broad definition of terrorism.
- Third, its sheer *volume*.
- And fourth, the significant *opposition* this legislation has engendered among all segments of civil society.

A more ominous trait is the potential threat that new laws have posed to the current status of freedom and liberty as transcendent values in Western liberal democracies.

The fundamental question is, "Are all these new laws necessary?" Wouldn't more rigorous enforcement of existing legislation have filled the bill, at least in Canada? During the process, parliamentarians were constantly told that this was *not* emergency legislation.

> A more ominous trait is the potential threat that new laws have posed to the current status of freedom and liberty.

Yet it was subject to closure in the Commons and time constraints in the Senate. When a splendid all-party special committee of the Senate was established to review the bill in a pre-study, I relaxed, confident that the committee would bring in strong recommendations. It did, after meeting nonstop for a week or two, after hearing three federal cabinet ministers and 30 witnesses. It reached consensus in recommending changes to safeguard our human rights and civil liberties.

However, when the bill came in formally on December 10, 2001, the proceedings were a charade. Everybody knew what would be allowed by a government with a huge majority in both Houses. When push came to shove, the all-party committee's recommendations were largely ignored. The bill passed with few amendments.

Bluntly put, Canada caved in to American demands, and therefore did not permit a full democratic process and debate to take place. The

~
**Bluntly put, Canada caved in to American demands, and therefore did not permit a full democratic process and debate to take place.**
~

government could not accept the majority of the amendments recommended by its own Senate committee without finding itself among those defined by President Bush as "against us."

## Using the United Nations as a rationale

The government used, as its rationale for this legislation, the security of the person. It cited the need for implementation of 12 international UN agreements that date back to 1963. All 12 provide legal tools to combat international terrorism.

I agree with that rationale. It is important to acknowledge these UN international resolutions. But the urgency with which Canada embraced them raises a question. Why should the government hasten to pass this legislation when Western democracies, and Canada in particular (including its provinces), have been so reluctant to implement *other* United Nations resolutions and actions, such as the UN Covenant on Economic, Social, and Cultural Rights?

When Canada last reported to the UN Human Rights Committee, our government was roundly criticized for not taking legislative action to ensure the rights of welfare people, single mothers, aboriginal people and others had been put in place, although we had pledged to do so by signing the covenant.

This non-implementation is based either on apathy (it assumes that the public neither know nor care about these UN covenants) or on a misplaced perception that these covenants merely state policy goals. Indeed one provincial premier has stated that Canada would never have signed these covenants if signing implied implementation! And Premier Harris of Ontario claimed that since *he* never signed on, he would not implement any of the covenants.

In the Fall of 2001 a long-awaited Senate Human Rights Committee was appointed to look at the Canada's record of implementation of the six main UN Covenants:

- the Covenant on Civil and Political Rights,
- the Convention on the Elimination of Discrimination against Women,
- the Convention on the Elimination of Racial Discrimination,
- the Convention on the Rights of the Child,
- the Covenant on Economic, Social, and Cultural Rights, and
- the Convention on the Rights of Migrant Workers and their Families.

None of these are well known by the public. There is therefore little pressure to pass Canadian legislation to implement these conventions and covenants domestically. My main work in the Senate has been to support the work of this newly established committee, and to put machinery in place to monitor and evaluate Canada's record of implementation. The first report of the Senate Committee on Human Rights, called *Promises to Keep*, recommended that the government assign sufficient resources to conduct a human rights impact analysis of the new security and counterterrorism measures.

## Response to pressure

My educated guess is that Canadian anti-terrorist legislation was a direct response to pressure from the United States and other Western allies. Politically, it was acceptable to a large part of the population in the grip of group-think and conformism, continuously stoked by fear and anger.

Because of this response, in the future Canada will be more dependent on the United States than ever before. It raises the question of how this country can stay Canadian.

The new security legislation has eroded freedom of choice and put limits to hard-won human rights. It is part, it seems to me, of an attitude that does not want to annoy the Americans on any issues. Don't push them on the Landmines Treaty, the International Criminal Court, the Kyoto

> **The new security legislation has eroded freedom of choice and put limits to hard-won human rights.**

Agreement on Climate Change, the missile defense system proposed for all of North America, or the treatment of prisoners in Cuba. Don't offend them by raising a clear Canadian voice.

It *is* tricky to know how to say "no" – particularly to the proposed missile defense system – because it is supposed to ensure security for us as well. If we don't raise our voices, however, we will lose all credibility in arms control talks internationally.

Canada has responsibility for our northern waters in the Arctic, where the U.S.A. has strategic interests. It is becoming clear that climate change is having a major effect on those northern waters. The federal government is preparing citizens for the huge economic costs to cope with the climatic implications, but I have seen nothing yet on the implications for humans. Aboriginal communities in the far north will have to be moved; dams will become ineffective either because of a huge rush of water caused by melting ice, or water flows will diminish to a trickle. How can Canada protect our people in the north, while falling into step with U.S. military defense plans?

All of this raises the need to rethink our understanding of security.

## A new understanding of security.

"What are we doing today that we, or our children, are going to find ourselves having to apologize for in a few years time?" asked syndicated columnist Richard Gwyn in the *Toronto Star*. He suggests two answers: the growing gap between the rich and the poor, and the demise of democracy.

~
**Is democracy synonymous with a market economy, as we are constantly being told?**
~

Both are related to the need for a new understanding of security.

President Bush exhorted people to get out and shop. Keeping consumers secure is paramount to growth. So economic security becomes a major objective. But is democracy synonymous with a market economy, as we are constantly being told? I think not. Yet the economic integration of North America hurtles on, and Thomas d'Aquino of the Business

Council on National Issues rejoices, "Everything we once hoped might happen is already happening."

An editorial comment in the *Globe and Mail* offered a contrary view: "We can [either] make the world safe for Western consumerism, or we can remake the economy to make it safe for the world."

Clearly, there is no shared vision of a sustainable society that is fair and equitable for all humans, for other species, and for future generations.

Now that the figures are in, we know that 40 percent of the casualties at the World Trade Center were *not* American. Many other countries were affected; no single country can guarantee security for all. Canadians are just as vulnerable as other humans.

> Globalization has weakened the structures of national governments, making any kind of supposed security for nation states questionable.

So what are the security issues for *humans,* rather than just for artificial entities called nations?

An emerging one, I suggest, is water. The need for this increasingly scarce resource is climbing high on the list of security needs. Who has water? Who needs it? What are they prepared to do to get it? What are the possible terms for sharing?

Environment is another issue. If there is no agreement on protecting the environment, who is going to survive? What value will protection of jobs have, if environmental change decimates populations of consumers? What good is a Gross National Product, if the nation is flooded by rising sea levels or people die because of pollution?

## The need for political change

Globalization has weakened the structures of national governments, making any kind of supposed security for nation states questionable. The logic of globalization is against national security. There are no longer any guarantees of security, as traditionally understood. If security really matters, why are we also rushing ahead with various free trade and investment agreements? And why are we at the same time contradicting the intent of those agreements by synchronizing immigration procedures with the U.S.A. in order to keep people out?

No country to my knowledge has looked at the need for co-operative *human* security through the building of relationships of trust. Nor has any country committed itself to the need for *restorative* justice over retributive justice. No wonder. In the current climate, dissent or deviation from group-think is not tolerated. Michael McGonicle, professor of law at Victoria University, charged in the *Globe and Mail* that "our own governments are making war on civil rights and public debate." As a cause, he cited "the erosion of civil liberties, the aggressive rhetoric of 'us against them,' and the uncloaked enthusiasm for raw military power."

Canada has given active leadership in the G20 group of nations, and hosted the G8 Summit in 2002. We have built the Human Security Network internationally. We gave a lead on the International Criminal Court, the Landmines Treaty, the Child Soldiers issue.

Politics is – unfortunately – a game in which winning is all, and the most powerful players are the prime minister, staff, and cabinet ministers. But do unprecedented and vast new arbitrary powers, indeed almost unlimited power, have to be given to cabinet ministers? The Justice Minister can now issue a certificate to block indefinitely the disclosure in court of any information the minister thinks could be detrimental to international relations, defense, or security.

I asked in the Senate Committee what I could do to have my name removed from a list of suspected terrorists, should my name ever appear. I was told I could write to the Solicitor General.

But then what, I asked, if I received a response that my name was not going to be removed from the list.

Well then, the answer was, I could go to court. What private citizen can afford to go to court against the bottomless pockets of government?

But if I did, what if the Justice Minister decided the information about me could be detrimental to international relations, defense, or security, and blocked the disclosure of that information? How then do I get justice in court?

## Undermining the possibility of dissent

This obsession with protecting information also lies behind the proposal to establish what amounts to secret trials for people charged under the anti-terrorism act, without seeing the evidence against them. It sounds to me like a Kafka novel. Do police powers have to be expanded? They no longer need to demonstrate that wiretapping is a last resort in probing terrorists; their maximum eavesdropping time has increased from 60 days to one year.

Efforts to conquer cells of terrorism will of course require reprisals. There will have to be preventive security at airports and at public gatherings. Nobody disputes that. And intelligence gathering assumes heightened importance, as does a means of stopping the money laundering that supports terrorism.

But do the new anti-terrorist laws strike an appropriate balance between affording security against terrorism to people on the one hand, and protecting hard-won and cherished civil liberties on the other? There is no immediate answer, although the debate will go on for a long time.

> There is no doubt in my mind that governments have exploited the events of September 11 for their own benefit.

There is no doubt in my mind that governments have exploited the events of September 11 for their own benefit, to entrench themselves more firmly in power. Consider the shaky support George W. Bush had before September 11, in contrast to what he now enjoys. Certainly the crisis was used by security and police forces to get powers they have long wanted. Western democracies such as Canada ingratiated themselves with the powerful Americans, by keeping up appearances and getting the legislation "through by Christmas."

President Bush has already abandoned the Anti-Ballistic Missile Treaty, is pushing his National Defense System (or second Star Wars), and wants Canada and others to support him in offensives against his so-called "axis of evil" – Iraq, Iran, and North Korea. He is pressing Canada to coordinate its refugee and visa policy with the Americans – to create a band of steel around the North American continent.

America is attempting to control the global agenda by militarizing it and by taking control of space as well. Our experience tells us that an isolationist security for North America will not work. But the new cross-border security pact will require Canada to give the FBI information on Canadian citizens that is protected by our own privacy laws. We shouldn't have to barter fundamental rights of privacy for continued access to the continental market.

Does the good life require a fair and equitable sharing of resources for all? Or are resources reserved for the few who control economic and political decisions – not just on defense issues, but on economic matters that affect everyone in North America?

If we are unwilling to deal with these matters, they will be dealt with for us.

## Restoring confidence

Terrorism, in other words, is not so much a security problem as a political problem. Confidence in the political system, nationally and internationally, needs to be restored in the public mind. The strong-arm tactics of the current government in rushing security legislation through has further eroded the declining trust of citizens in government. With the current cynicism about politics, who will take on the formidable task of restoring credibility to the political process?

**Terrorism, in other words, is not so much a security problem as a political problem.**

Confidence in the UN and its instruments also needs to be restored. Advocacy for the international rule of law is desperately needed. Currently the international community risks having too narrow a focus on security, and too little focus on human rights.

Let me suggest some characteristics of what I believe good governance will require.

1. Good governance will need to *guarantee and encourage citizen participation*. Voting every four years does not a democracy make! The erection of fences, the declaration

~

Let me suggest some characteristics of what I believe good governance will require.

~

of special military zones to exclude civilians, and the refusal to amend legislation in response to public outcry does not encourage citizen participation. If the same amount of energy and hard work were invested in exchange and dialogue as is presently invested in planning for tear gas and riot squads we might see some fruitful results.

2. Good governance has to demonstrate *accountability to people for their collective good*. We claim to do this in Canada through elected representatives. But how accountable are they? I am appointed, not elected, but you might be surprised by the number of requests for assistance I receive because a particular member of parliament didn't or wouldn't act.

    Both the House of Commons and the Senate need reform. Probably the Commons could adopt a modified proportional representation system and then the Senate could be shaped around that new reality. Either an effective opposition, or effective checks and balances on power, is essential to democracy.

    Social reformers (I'm thinking here of nongovernment organizations and churches) need to examine and redefine their strategies. Petitions simply get noted and filed. The effectiveness of individual letters is uncertain. Lobbying should be done with members of the sitting government as well as the opposition. Demonstrations may unite a group, but rarely lead to fundamental change in policy. Both Government and NGOs need to find ways of including the poor in fundamental social change.

3. Good governance has to *protect human rights*, balancing the safety of the person with civil liberties. Civil and political rights are interdependent with economic, social, and cultural rights. Military victories will not ensure security if people have nothing to eat.

4. Good governance demands *a free flow of information and a critical mindset*. Access to information and the right to dissent are essential in a free democratic society. When public consultations are planned, governments, corporations, and nongovernment organizations all need to be told. A free flow of information also demands a press no longer satisfied with simply recycling press releases.

5. Finally, Canada needs to develop *a consensus on "national vision"* because Canadians are divided by the values that they currently espouse. Civil society needs to turn from protest to vision, and to work with government to articulate and define such a vision.

## Looking into the future

On my darkest days I see a world bereft of community and plagued with loss of ultimate meaning as a result of September 11, 2001.

On my more optimistic days I see a community of nations, building a common human security, based on the just sharing of needed resources, in a fashion geared to long-term sustainability. Everyone has a right to the basics of existence and to ultimate meaning in their lives. On my brightest days I see more political transparency gained by the exposure of the lies and hypocrisy of the rich and powerful. I see an exercise of political power that demonstrates its role, not in domination of the outsider and the weak, but by facilitating a vision of a shared future for all.

The Indian philosopher Radhakrishnan called the "supreme task of our generation to give a soul to our growing world consciousness." September 11 might just be the event that shakes our complacency and gets us at it.

# 6

# The prerequisite for peace

## Keith Wright

We have heard it said repeatedly, "Life will never be the same after September 11th." Certainly, life has changed drastically and dramatically since that fateful morning. Various facets of that change are the subject of this book. I believe that one of the greatest changes lies in our perception of religion.

Religion has always had a dark side, an abusive side. History is replete with examples of religious abuse – the Crusades of the 12th through the 14th centuries, the Inquisition, the Holy Wars in Europe, and the Witch Hunts of New England come to mind immediately. However, the attack on the World Trade Center and the Pentagon represented a quantum leap in public awareness of this dark side of religion. Before our eyes in ghastly images on the television screen, the reality of religious extremism was exposed in a way that cannot be expunged from our memories.

September 11 represented a religious awakening for many people. Unfortunately, for some it was only a partial awakening. It is easy to see the fault in someone else's religion but more difficult to recognize the failings of one's own faith.

### An exclusive focus

In this partial awakening, some people could see clearly how a particular interpretation of one religion, Islam, had turned its followers into warriors and avengers for Allah. Osama bin Laden and his fellow terrorists believed that Allah was offended by the materialism and decadence of the West and particularly America. They were outraged by the way in which American economic and military might had kept corrupt governments in power in Arab countries and allowed an American presence in lands that are sacred to Islam. Obviously, bin Laden's grievances with America were also fueled by considerations that went beyond religion, but there was no escaping the part that religion played in shaping his hatred of what he and his followers called "The Great Satan."

**The abuse of exclusivity is present in every religion.**

This partial awakening focused on those within Islam who twisted the teachings of the Koran to sanction the taking of innocent lives as a warning to those whom they were convinced were leading the followers of Allah astray. That is obviously a starting place in identifying religious abuse but it is woefully inadequate if the awakening does not go further and recognize that the abuse of exclusivity is present in every religion, including one's own. And the awakening will be incomplete if it concentrates solely on the more violent manifestations of abuse that are so obvious in terrorism and in bloody conflicts in many places around the world.

Our wake-up call begins, then, with a summons to repudiate the claim that a saving relationship with God can be found only in one religion and only in one understanding of that religion. Exclusivity has built barriers and obstacles which make it impossible for people to learn from each other and to live together in harmony and peace. Therefore, we must challenge those in every religion who proclaim that God is revealed solely through their religion and that God condemns those who approach God in other ways.

### Learning to criticize ourselves

Recently, an article appeared on the editorial page of the *Austin American-Statesman* entitled "Muslims Should Try Introspection." It was written by a Muslim, Mona Ettahawy, who was a journalist in Egypt for ten years. Ms. Ettahawy called for liberal, moderate, and progressive Muslims to speak out. She wrote, "We've been quiet too long, and I blame us for the sad state of affairs of the Muslim Umma (community) as much as I blame the clerics, whom, I must admit, I gave up on long ago." Ms. Ettahawy continued, "About 10 years ago, I went through a crisis of faith that swept away lazy answers and made me realize how much work it takes to keep my faith viable. For inspiration, I turned to Muslim scholars whom I considered revolutionaries. They were reinterpreting Islam by looking it squarely with modern eyes. They dared to utter the R-word – Reformation."

Ms. Ettahawy's call for introspection needs to be echoed in every faith tradition. It is especially needed in the religion of which I am a part, Christianity. For much too long Christians have been the ultimate exclusivists. Christians have approached people of other religions with an arrogance and imperialism that

> **For much too long Christians have been the ultimate exclusivists.**

is shameful. We dismissed the religious traditions of the native people of North and South America as mere superstition, never bothering to understand their beliefs. We stole their land and took away their faith, in the name of civilizing people we regarded as savages – sometimes "noble savages" but savages nonetheless. We sent missionaries to many countries to convert the people of other religions to Christianity in the firm belief that those of other faiths were doomed to hell if they did not profess Christ as their Savior.

And, while we were trying to convert adherents of other religions to Christianity, exclusivity manifested itself in our relationship with other Christians. We have a long history of fighting among ourselves, with one group or the other of Christians claiming to have the true faith and branding everyone else as heretics. For centuries the Roman Catholic Church taught that there was no salvation outside the mother church. This meant that Protestants were all condemned to Hell. Only recently has the Roman dogma *extra ecclesiam nulla salus* (outside the church, no salvation) been rescinded. Protestants have been equally narrow in claiming that Roman Catholics were unsaved.

## The origins of anti-Semitism

Our exclusivity has revealed itself in many ways. But nowhere has it been more disastrous than in our relationship with our spiritual ancestors, the Jews. Just recently, the Pope went to Israel to ask forgiveness for the Roman Catholic Church's failure to protest the atrocities committed by Nazi Germany against the Jewish People. Lutherans would have done well to join the Pope in that visit, because Martin Luther wrote a tract which could have served as a blueprint for Hitler's "final solution." Luther thought that Jews would flock to the Protestant Church after he broke with Rome. When they did not, he vented his rage in a pamphlet entitled "On the Jews and their Lies." In that pamphlet, distributed in 1543, he spelled out a program for dealing with the Jews that Adolph Hitler carried out to the letter 400 years later. This was what he wrote:

> First, set fire to their synagogues or schools.
>
> Second, I advise that their houses be razed and destroyed.
>
> Third, I advise that all their prayer books and Talmudic writings, in which such adulteries, lies, cursing and blasphemy are taught, to be taken from them.
>
> Fourth, I advise that their Rabbis be forbidden to teach henceforth on pain of loss of life and limb.
>
> Fifth, I advise that safe-conduct on the highways be abolished completely for the Jews.
>
> Sixth, I advise that ... all cash and treasure of silver and gold be taken from them.
>
> Seventh ... throw brimstone and pitch upon them, so much the better ... and if this is not enough, let them be driven like mad dogs out of the land.

The atrocities of the Holocaust were simply the culmination of centuries of anti-Semitism nurtured and encouraged by Christians who blamed the Jews for the death of Christ and taught that there was no salvation for God's chosen people. Understandably, then, when

Christians became aware of the horrors of the death camps, they backed the creation of the State of Israel as a form of penitence for past sins against the Jews.

Actually, the conception and planning for a Jewish state had begun many years before the United Nations voted on November 29, 1947, to partition Palestine into Jewish and Arab sectors. In the end, however, it was enormous emotional and political support from the United States that persuaded the UN to act. And once again the creation of Israel was seen in the Arab World as an act of Western imperialism.

> ~
>
> **The atrocities of the Holocaust were simply the culmination of centuries of anti-Semitism nurtured and encouraged by Christians who blamed the Jews for the death of Christ.**
>
> ~

The sin of anti-Semitism could not be atoned for simply by confiscating land from Arab Muslims and Christians. Consequently, we planted the seeds of the political and religious conflict that rages in Palestine today, a conflict that had direct impact on the events of September 11.

## Challenging our exclusivity

Obviously, the introspection that Ms. Ettahawy called for in the Muslim religion is desperately needed in the Christian faith as well. We need pastors, theologians, and informed lay people who are willing to challenge the exclusivity that has dominated our faith for centuries. We need people like Joseph C. Hough, Jr., the president of Union Seminary in New York. In an interview printed in the *New York Times*, Dr. Hough said,

> ...a new Christian theology of religions will involve the recognition that the fomenting of religious conflict has been and still is a theological problem for Christians, because we have made our claim to God's revelation exclusively ours. Our history of internal conflict and persecution of persons

of other religions is a grim reminder that we have killed each other and members of other religions in defending that exclusive claim. Ironically, by the defense of our exclusionary claim, we have often lived a contradiction of the spirit of Jesus Christ.[1]

Hough goes on to say in this interview, "I am a Christian who strongly believes that God has always been and now is working everywhere in every human culture to redeem the world. I believe that there is ample evidence in the best of the world's religions, including our own, that God's work is effective. Muslims, Jews, Hindus, Buddhists and others have been and are being transformed by a powerful vision of God that redeems them with hope and infuses their religious practice with compassion, justice and peace."

## Addressing the doctrine of atonement

In his interview, Dr. Hough called for a "new theology of religions." I am convinced that that any such new theology must address the Doctrine of the Atonement if we are ever going to move beyond our present exclusivity. Christians are exclusivists because we have been taught that Christ's death on the cross was a sacrifice offered to God to satisfy God's honor or to pay the penalty for our sins, *and that salvation depends upon our accepting the atoning work of Christ.*

> Theology must address the Doctrine of the Atonement if we are ever going to move beyond our present exclusivity.

If this is a correct understanding of what God was doing in Christ's death on the cross, we must remain an exclusive religion obligated to proclaim that there is only one way to salvation. And if we really are concerned that people be saved from the fires of hell, we will be diligent to see that any who lead others astray with false teachings are silenced, removed, or destroyed. This reasoning led John Calvin, a leader in the Reformation, to consent to the murder of Servitus, a man whom the

Reformer believed was teaching a false doctrine in the city of Geneva where Calvin had been asked to be the spiritual leader.

To move beyond exclusivity, Christians must take a long, hard look at the prevailing understanding of the atonement to see if it really reflects the message of the Bible and God's intent for humanity. And that examination, it seems to me, must begin with a reappraisal of our understanding of God. The most popular understanding of the atonement, the understanding of the atonement that is found in our creedal statements, is based on a perception of God as King, Lord, Ruler, Judge – a righteous, pure, and holy being who insists upon perfect obedience and unswerving loyalty.

Thus the object of Jesus' sacrificial death is to satisfy the justice of the All-Righteous One or to appease the anger of the offended Potentate or Ruler.

## Transforming our picture of God

However, that picture of God does not square with the image of God reflected in the life and teachings of Jesus. When we stop to examine the parables and instructions of Jesus, we find that he portrays God most often as "Father." When his disciples asked him to teach them to pray, Jesus gave them a model for their praying which begins, "Our Father…"

Hans Küng, a Roman Catholic theologian, points out how revolutionary was Jesus' choice of "Father" for addressing God in this prayer. There are isolated instances in which God is referred to as Father in the Old Testament. But Jesus' use of the Aramaic form *abba* for "Father" in speaking to God is extraordinary. Küng comments,

> *Abba* – like our "Daddy" – is originally a child's word, used however in Jesus' time also as a form of address to their father by grown-up sons and daughters and as an expression of politeness generally to older persons deserving of respect. But to use this not particularly manly expression of tenderness, drawn from the child's vocabulary, this

commonplace term of politeness, to use this as a form of addressing God, must have struck Jesus' contemporaries as irreverent and offensively familiar, very much as if we were to address God today as "Dad."[2]

Jesus was changing his disciples' concept of God. Completely absent from the salutation of this prayer are the terms of obeisance and honor and glory that one would expect if one were addressing the King of Heaven, the Lord of the Universe. We are given a different image of God. As Küng puts it, "He is not the all-too-masculine God of arbitrary power or law. He is not the God created in the image of kings and tyrants, of hierarchs and schoolmasters. But he is the good God – it is difficult to find less trite formulas – who identifies himself with men, with their needs and hopes. He does not demand but gives, does not oppress but raises up, does not wound but heals."[3]

One of Jesus' most well-known parables completes the transformation of God's image. In the Parable of the Prodigal Son, God is pictured as the father who gives his younger son his inheritance when the son asks for it, who watches sadly as the son leaves but does not chase after him, who sees the son returning and runs out to meet him and finally, interrupting his son's admission of guilt, accepts him back without question or demanding a period of probation and orders his servants to prepare a great feast.

> **The God whom Jesus reveals is not the righteous judge or outraged potentate that atonement theories have painted for us.**

The God whom Jesus reveals is a God of infinite, inexhaustible love – not the righteous judge or outraged potentate that atonement theories have painted for us. In this insight, Native Americans could have taught the missionaries who came to convert them. In the book, *A Native American Theology*, the authors tell us, "There is no sense in any Native traditions that reflect any attempt to make God, a god, or the spirits, happy with us or to placate the judgment of God over against a sinful humanity. There is no sense of God's anger. In fact, the notion of Wakonda cannot conceive of ascribing human emotions to Wakonda."[4]

The authors go on to say, "There were ceremonies to make right an imbalance that we ourselves as pitiful two-leggeds may have instigated – through our laziness, inattention, oversight, anger, or some unknown mistake. But even in such cases, the anger of the spirits is never at stake in most Native traditions when those traditions are understood at their most complex level."[5]

## A God who breaks down hostilities

When we discover the God whom Jesus came to reveal, we realize that the objective of Jesus' birth, life, teachings, actions, death, and resurrection is to draw us back to our heavenly parent rather than to pay off a wrathful king or an all-righteous judge. As we grasp this new understanding of the atonement, we realize that throughout all of history, God has been seeking to reconcile an alienated humanity to our Creator in order that we can become more nearly what we were created to be. Who Jesus is and what Jesus does is aimed at changing something in us rather than changing something in God.

> God has been active in every culture, in every religion, in every place on the earth, breaking down the walls of hostility that separate us from each other.

And with this new insight, it should dawn upon us that God has been active in every culture, in every religion, in every place on the earth, breaking down the walls of hostility that prevent us from being whole and healthy and that separate us from each other and the ultimate source of our being. I find it inconceivable that this God of great compassion and infinite love would choose to reveal God's love to a tiny fraction of the people of the world and ignore the rest of humanity.

Exclusivity makes God a narrow, loveless being that simply cannot be squared with the God who is revealed in the Hebrew/Christian scriptures and all of the other great religions of the world. It is time for scholars, theologians, religious leaders, and informed lay people to take a hard look at the concept of God that spawned our doctrine of the atonement and ultimately the exclusivity that has brought such great conflict and suffering to our world.

## The shadow side of religions

September 11 forced us to look at the bloodiest aspect of religious abuse, but we would do well to let this awakening take us further in our examination of the shadow side of religion. Religion, like every institution in which humans are involved, is ambivalent. It blesses but it also curses. It has taught great truths but it also has misled people badly. It has created communities of refuge and encouragement but it has also torn families and regions and nations apart. It brings comfort and peace to many but it also brings fear and a great burden of guilt to others.

> Religion, like every institution in which humans are involved, is ambivalent. It blesses but it also curses.

If we concentrate solely on the negative side of religion, we may end up throwing the baby out with the bath water. We may rob ourselves of the great blessing that a religious community can bring to us. But if we acknowledge only the positive side of religion, we leave ourselves vulnerable to the wounds which religion can inflict upon us personally, and what may be even worse, we fail to demand the changes in our religious communities which will make them less abusive for others.

So, the awful tragedy that woke us up can lead beyond its initial revelation to a deeper exploration of the dark side of religion. Let me start you on that exploration by suggesting one particular abuse that illustrates how religion can hurt as well as heal. There are many other ways that religion can be abusive and I hope that you will be stimulated to look further, but let us begin by looking at the abuse of women.

We have been horrified by the reports of how the Taliban in Afghanistan abused women and justified what they have done as a part of their Islamic faith. And so we should be. However, it is the height of inconsistency to criticize the actions of the Taliban without examining the treatment of women in other religions and especially in the Christian faith. Women have not fared well in any of the great religions of the world and Christianity is no exception.

## Raising the status of women

Both Mohammed and Jesus can be credited with raising the status of women in their own time. Huston Smith, the author of one of the most respected books on world religions, rejects the accusation often heard in the West that Islam degrades women. He says, "If we approach the question historically, comparing the status of Arabian women before and after Mohammed, the charge is patently false. In the pre-Islamic 'days of ignorance' marriage arrangements were so loose as to be scarcely recognizable. Women were regarded as little more than chattel, to be done with as fathers or husbands pleased. Daughters had no inheritance rights and were often buried alive in their infancy."[6]

Smith goes on to show the how the teachings of the Koran addressed many of the abuses suffered by women before the time of Mohammed. He says,

> The Koranic reforms improved woman's status incalculably. They forbade infanticide. They required that daughters be included in inheritance – not equally, it is true, but to half the proportion of sons ... In her rights as citizen – education, suffrage, and vocation – the Koran leaves open the possibility of woman's full equality with man, an equality that is being approximated as the customs of Muslim nations become modernized. It was in the institution of marriage, however, that Islam made its greatest contribution to women. It sanctified marriage, first, by making it the sole lawful locus of the sexual act. Second, the Koran requires that a woman give her free consent before she may be wed ... Third, Islam tightened the wedding bond enormously.[7]

Just as Mohammed elevated the status of women, so did Jesus change the perception of women. Women were included among Jesus' followers,

> ∿
> ## Just as Mohammed elevated the status of women, so did Jesus change the perception of women.
> ∿

something unheard of in the time in which he lived. Jesus dared to speak to the woman at the well in Samaria, breaking both the prohibition of a man addressing a woman in public and a Jew having any kind of contact with a Samaritan. Marcus Borg, who has spent much of his life studying the life of Jesus, speaks of Jesus' revolutionary way of relating to women when he says,

> The role of women in the Jesus movement is striking. The stories of Jesus' interaction with women are remarkable. They range from his defense of the woman who outraged an all-male banquet not only by entering it but also by (unveiled and with hair unbraided) washing his feet with her hair, to his being hosted by Mary and Martha and affirming Mary's role as disciple, to his learning from a Syro-Phoenician Gentile woman. Women were apparently part of the itinerant group traveling with Jesus. Indeed, they were apparently among his most devoted followers, as the stories of their presence at his death suggests. The movement itself was financially supported by some wealthy women. Moreover, the evidence is compelling that women played leadership roles in the Post-Easter community."[8]

## Letting the vision down

We must give Jesus and Mohammed credit for elevating the status of women over what existed in their time. But we must go on to say that the religions which they inspired did not challenge the fundamental inequality that existed and continues to exist between men and women. Christianity and Islam are still patriarchal religions, dominated and controlled by men who continue to insist that God intended that women be subservient to men. Most Christians still portray God as a male deity whose chief characteristic is power and authority. Only in the most recent times have some Protestant denominations allowed women to serve as pastors or officers, and the Roman Catholic Church continues to prohibit women from serving as priests. The advances in rights and privileges that Western women have made in the last century are due more to industrialization and democracy than they are to the influence of the dominant religion, Christianity.

> The advances in rights and privileges that Western women have made in the last century are due more to industrialization and democracy than they are to Christianity.

Once again it is time for scholars, theologians, clergy, and informed lay people to take the lead in insisting on changes in thinking and practices that will restore women to their God-given equality with men. And in this case, the three great religions which share a common scripture could work together to provide the scholarship and insights that would expose the errors in biblical interpretation that have caused such misery and suffering for women for hundreds of years.

As I suggest in my book, *Religious Abuse*, that investigation must begin with pivotal texts in the first three chapters of Genesis. According to the biblical account, God crowned creation by bringing into being *both* men and women. The long-standing translation of Genesis 1:26 is misleading. What most people have heard all of their lives is "Then God said, 'Let us make *man* in our image.'" A more accurate translation is, "Then God said, 'Let us make *humankind* in our image.'" There is no doubt that this is the intent when we go on to verse 27, which says, "So God created humankind in God's image, in the image of God, God created them; *male and female* God created them."

In the beginning, the ancient writer says, both men and women were created in the image of God, and both were given the task of being co-creators with God and stewards of all that God had made.

But there is another textual hurdle to surmount. In Genesis 3:16, we read that God said to the first woman, Eve, "Your desire shall be for your husband, and he shall rule over you." That seems to make it very clear that God intends that men be dominant and women subservient.

~

**We will meet resistance from many, including those clergy and other religious leaders who have a vested interest in maintaining the status quo.**

~

However, theologian Johanna W. H. Van Wijk-Bos argues that this was not God's intention at all. Rather, it was the consequence of human mistrust and our refusal to live as God had intended. The third chapter of Genesis is a parable to help us understand our brokenness and alienation, not only from God but from each other. God is not, in this verse, declaring what God *intended* for the relationship between men and women. Rather God is describing how things will be in a broken world.

Wijk-Bos points the way back to wholeness when she says,

> The complementing contrast to this text is Galatians 3:28: "There is neither Jew nor Greek, there is neither slave nor free, *there is neither male nor female*, for you are all one in Christ Jesus" (RSV). Here the new creation is announced as a fulfillment of what the creation was intended to be.[9]

God's intention is not domination/subservience; it is mutuality between men and women. It is that intention which leaders in all three Abrahamic religions must hold before us as the ideal toward which we must strive in minimizing abuse and building the world God envisions.

## An opportunity to promote peace

Good often comes from tragedy. That will be the case if September 11 opens our eyes to the many forms that religious abuse takes and causes us to work together to minimize those abuses and build healthier religions.

It will not be easy. We will meet resistance from many, including those clergy and other religious leaders who have a vested interest in maintaining the status quo. But it must be done if we are to find the peace and security that we all desire.

That is particularly true of the abuse of exclusivity. Hans Küng reminds us of this fact when he says, "I became increasingly aware that discussion with other world religions is actually essential for survival, necessary for the sake of peace in the world."[10] Then he adds, "Peace among the religions is the prerequisite for peace among the nations."

## Endnotes

[1] *New York Times*, Jan. 12, 2001, Sec A-19.

[2] Hans Küng, *On Being a Christian*, (New York: Doubleday & Company, 1974), p. 315.

[3] Ibid, p. 312.

[4] Clara Sue Kidwell, Homer Noley, George E. Tinker, *A Native American Theology*, (New York: Orbis Books, 2001), p. 64.

[5] Ibid, p. 65.

[6] Huston Smith, *The World's Religions*, (New York: HarperSanFrancisco, 1991), p. 251.

[7] Ibid, p. 251.

[8] Marcus Borg, *Meeting Jesus Again for the First Time: The Historical Jesus and the Heart of the Contemporary Faith*, (San Francisco: HarperSanFrancisco, 1994), p. 57.

[9] Johanna W. H. Van Wijk-Bos, *Reformed and Feminist*, (Louisville: Westminster/John Knox Press, 1991), p. 66.

[10] Hans Küng, *Theology for the Third Millennium: An Ecumenical View*, (New York: Doubleday, 1988), p. 227.

# 7

# What September 11 taught me about preaching

## William Willimon

You know us preachers. We complain that no one listens to what we preach. They sit there in the pews, with our little words bouncing off their hard heads, ricocheting off the walls. Then the words die and are heard no more.

But not on the Sunday after Tuesday. For a time, at least, it seemed as if everybody had to be a theologian, whether one wanted to be a theologian or not, as those people in the pews asked, "God, why?"

But many of us found that one had to be a theologian within certain restraints. It is socially acceptable to ask, "Why?" To be a bit more specific – in our cultural context, it is quite conventional to ask, "Why did this happen to *me?*"

What is risky and potentially unacceptable are the possible answers to that question. In preaching, to ask "*God*, why?" is to risk the possibility of address, confrontation, a word not of our own devising, a word from God. And that can be downright uncomfortable.

In the face of a devastating national crisis, we wanted more than a word from God. We wanted a word that would help us pull together, to move as one. Some word that might take away some of the pain. A word that helped us present a united front against the enemy.

Thus, in the week after Tuesday, we experienced two conflicting tendencies.

On the one hand, we were desperate for a word, an answer, to the question, *Why?* In 30 years of ministry, I do not recall seeing people so desperate for words. In the days following Tuesday, I had calls from the BBC, NBC, and from a number of local news stations, all curious about what clergy were saying. The *New York Times*, not noted for its religion coverage, reprinted excerpts from sermons around the city the next week.

A great trauma makes theologians of us all. In the face of so massive a tragedy, we become desperate for the Word. More than one fellow

> ~
> ## A great trauma makes theologians of us all.
> ~

preacher told me that, after spending a lifetime complaining that no one listens to preachers, it was truly terrifying suddenly to be thrust into a moment when everyone *wanted* to hear a sermon.

As I stood on the steps of our university chapel that Sunday, looking into the faces of those scurrying in – a good half-hour before the service was to begin – I saw on their faces desperation. And I – as the only person at the chapel that day who knew what the sermon intended to say – panicked.

## The pressure to conform

On the other hand, while people seemed desperately to want a word, there were plenty of indications that the word we wanted would be carefully policed.

"Politically incorrect" TV talk show host, Bill Maher, was severely censored for his rather flippant comments about the terrorists, saying that they were brave, crazy but brave, braver than the United States who merely sent unmanned missiles at our adversaries. Maher was forced to apologize profusely.

When newscaster Peter Jennings expressed the mildest of reservations about the President's rhetorical abilities, thousands of e-mails rebuked him.

It was a time for the country to unite, not a time for nay-saying. In a moment, we had all been rendered into victims – not just those of us in New York, but all Americans. A great injustice can produce a great sense of innocence among those who have suffered the injustice.

Innocence is particularly dangerous, particularly when it is felt among the powerful, because the powerful can be terribly destructive when they believe themselves to be innocent. When one is a pure victim, totally innocent, then all moral bets are off. Ships were sent to sea to guard Manhattan.

"Bomb 'em to hell," chanted a small group of students on Wednesday after a memorial service on our campus for the victims.

The service on Friday, after Tuesday, at the National Cathedral, appeared to set the tone for many services throughout the country. The service was relentlessly patriotic, with little word of judgment or even reservation expressed by the clergy. President Bush stood in the pulpit and called for all-out war and retribution. At Robert Schuller's "Crystal Cathedral," they unfurled the flag. And everyone seemed eager to stand and sing, "God Bless America." The predominate symbol for the week that stands out in everyone's mind was the American flag, not the Christian cross.

> The predominate symbol for the week that stands out in everyone's mind was the American flag, not the Christian cross.

I received an e-mail from a sophomore on Sunday evening, after what I thought had been a wonderful service in our chapel that morning. The student was "deeply disappointed" that there was hardly any mention of support for "our president," in the service and "even more disturbing, a total absence of our beloved flag. You politically correct clergy have failed to help us during our crisis," he complained.

I explained to the young man, as best I could, that this was church, not Yankee Stadium, that we have been given resources greater than innocuous TV platitudes like "unity," "together," and "forward." I told him that, on Sunday between eleven and noon, we had our hands full just trying to listen to Jesus, just bending our lives toward him. So there tended to be no energy left, by noon, for support of the president. It wasn't that the church and its clergy were "politically correct," it was just that we were strange. We hoped that it was following Jesus that made us that way.

I haven't seen him in the chapel since.

## Stretched between desires

As a young pastor in Switzerland, Karl Barth said that he felt stretched between the contemporary situation and the biblical text. How to speak a word between the two? "As ministers we ought to speak of God. We are human, however, and so cannot speak of God. We ought therefore to recognize both our obligation and our inability and by that very recognition give God glory."[1]

> When faced with so huge an event as September 11, the situation at the moment tended to elbow God out of the way.

Many of us preachers found that, when faced with so huge an event as September 11, the situation at the moment tended to elbow God out of the way. In Daytona Beach, Florida, at a large service that following Sunday, the preacher called for "massive and disproportionate retaliation" upon any nation that colludes with terrorists, saying that when the army caught terrorists, they ought to be executed on the spot. His comment was greeted, it was reported, with amens and hallelujahs.[2]

This is where we preachers come in. On Sunday after Tuesday it was our peculiar task, not simply to comfort a people in trauma, but to comfort in the name of Jesus Christ. Our business was not simply to offer a helpful word but a faithful one as well. Laying the story of the life, death, and resurrection of Jesus over the story of September 11 was our great challenge by September 16.

Soon after September 16, I began collecting sermons from campus pastors and college chaplains from around the country. I got over a hundred sermons which I eventually collected into a book, *The Sunday After Tuesday: Campus Pastors Respond to 9/11.*[3]

Here are a few of my impressions after collecting these sermons.

My first impression was that when congregations lacked substantive liturgical habits, they also lacked the theological means to resist the pressures of the moment. When, in great pain, we reached for a reassuring symbol, we grasped an American flag, not a chalice or a Bible. It is therefore probably not amazing that some sermons after 9/

11 offered mostly humanistic advice, patriotic suggestions for things that we can do to take away some of the pain, rather than reach for an affirmation about what God has done or is doing in the present crisis. Some sermons seemed greatly concerned to somehow account for all that God did *not* do in the crisis.

> When we reached for a reassuring symbol, we grasped an American flag, not a chalice or a Bible.

All of the sermons that I collected were preached by campus pastors, chaplains, or pastors who work with students. One characteristic of this generation of young adults is their ambivalence, or downright hostility, toward institutional, traditional embodiment of the faith. They tend to prefer something vaguely reassuring like "spirituality" to the more demanding, more specific orthodox Christian faith. So I was not surprised to find those who speak to them invoking the values of friendship, caring, volunteerism, and personal involvement rather than more theologically explicit commitments.

Yet many of the sermons really did try to stand under a biblical text, really struggled theologically with, "Is there any word from the Lord?" In so doing, they preached from an amazing diversity of texts. There were sermons on texts that ranged from the Tower of Babel to 1 Corinthians 13. For my own sermon that Sunday, I jettisoned the prescribed *Revised Common Lectionary* texts and went with Genesis 1.

Yet there is something to be said for those who stayed with a text prescribed by the lectionary on the Sunday after Tuesday, who let the text, rather than Tuesday, determine the thrust of the sermon. I found a peculiar delight in the sermons that, while clearly shaped by the events of the week, were not utterly determined by them, were not jerked around by either the terrorists or the politicians, and that went on and preached the great themes of the faith. This, in itself, became a kind of testimonial that the church, rather than the world, sets the agenda for the People of God.

## Making the church relevant again

Karl Barth, when he testified to how his mind had changed in an article for *The Christian Century* in 1939, almost apologetically explained that while he was busy doing theology, Hitler came on the scene. Hitler's ascendancy made it necessary for him, for the moment, to lay aside churchly concerns and become "*simultaneously,* very much more churchly *and* very much more worldly... For this change I am indebted to the Führer!"[4] Perhaps we preachers to young adults – thrust so suddenly to the forefront by a world demanding a word, by the rhetorical shortfall of the President, by the fury of the terrorists, by the bundle of feelings of hurt, hate, and loss – should have expressed our gratitude to the world for suddenly making the peculiar speech of the church once again a matter of life and death.

> ∼
> Perhaps we preachers should have expressed our gratitude to the world for suddenly making the peculiar speech of the church once again a matter of life and death.
> ∼

Our chapel was packed to capacity in the weeks after the tragedy on Tuesday. Since that time, as the war became almost routine, and the terrorist threat more diffused, the congregation dwindled to more typical proportions. What seemed on that first Sunday like a people turning desperately back to God, eventually became a people following the President's exhortation to get back to business as usual and shop our way to victory. Thus, I have been reminded in these past months that it is not an easy thing, certainly not a thing that comes naturally, to worship the true and living God.

> ∼
> I have been reminded in these past months that it is not an easy thing, certainly not a thing that comes naturally, to worship the true and living God.
> ∼

A friend of mine was briefly on a nationwide radio talk show, appearing there as a "Christian representative." When the show began, the interviewer turned to my friend and said, "Now you are a pastor. Tell us, what does your faith say about what we've been through?"

My friend cleared his throat and said something like, "Well, as Christians we are trying to follow Jesus, who forgave his enemies and refused to let us defend him. Jesus also teaches us that we are all sinners, even when we are wronged by others we are like them in our sin. So we ask God to forgive us and to help us see even our enemies as brothers and sisters in Christ."

"Thank you," said the host. Then he turned to the next guest with, "Rabbi, what does your faith say about what we've been through?"

"First, let me say that I totally disagree with what your first guest just said. That's terrible! We don't need this sort of wishy-washy forgiveness bit. We need strong response to these terrorists. That's all they understand. Those people who died were not 'sinners,' they were victims of inhuman aggression."

It's a time to be reminded of how very strange is the gospel.

It is a very peculiar thing to worship the true and living God, a God who comes to us as Trinity, a God who is a Jew from Nazareth. As one of the preachers in my collection of sermons put it, "I am a member of a religion that worships a Middle Eastern man." The Emory University professor who, as one of the endless TV interpreters of Islam, said, "Christians and Moslems all worship the same God," did not get it quite right. The same God may be a theoretical possibility but is not an actuality, if you care about being faithful to the Bible. Jesus does not easily mesh with Mohammed, no matter how much our need for national unity. There is a rather remarkable gulf between Islam and Christianity and, in deference to both faiths, that difference must be respected. One can only wonder what Osama bin Laden and his cohorts think of George Bush lecturing them on "true Islam."

## Out of the mouths of babes

A couple of Sundays after our fateful Tuesday, while attending a large downtown church, I noticed that the young children were entering the sanctuary for the service with bags marked "Worshipper in

Training." In our place, we called those same children's activity bags, full of crayons, Bible coloring books, etc., "Quiet Bags." I like better the designation "Worshipper in Training," not only for the children, but for us all. On any Sunday morning, in any church, all of us are constantly in training for the odd activity of worshipping a God of truth and light. Faithful Christian worship is always a challenge, but never so great as when we walk to church through the rubble of dashed dreams, crushed innocence, the end of the old world and the uncertain, even frightening beginning of the new.

My associate preached a sermon a couple of weeks later in which he told of a conversation with a Duke student. The student's little brothers, aged something like six and four, were being kept by their father on the Wednesday after Tuesday. The father was trying to baby-sit and listen to the television news at the same time. The TV announcer said that the President was going to address the nation in just a moment.

"Now you and your brother have got to be quiet because the most important person in the world is getting ready to speak!" said the father to the older of the two children.

The six-year-old turned and said to his brother, "You have got to be quiet now. God is about to speak to us."

Out of the mouths of babes!

## Therapy or judgment

It is not surprising that many of the sermons right after that fateful Tuesday were mostly in a therapeutic mode, including my own. Such a few days after the tragedy, people were still in acute pain and shock. It did not seem a time for prophetic judgment but a time for pastoral reassurance. What I found rather amazing is that a number of the sermons I read went right ahead and waded into matters of judgment. While their interpretations had more theological nuance than the early statements of Jerry Falwell or Pat Robertson, some of the preachers were so brash as to interpret the events that happened on September 11 as testimony to the sin, not only of the terrorists, but our sin as well.

Perhaps these campus pastors knew that there can be no real healing without truthful ministry to the cognitive dissonance that was felt by many after Tuesday. We were in a new world, not because of a Tuesday in New York, but because of a Friday in Jerusalem. Calvary required, and always does require, new thinking. And an integral part of any specifically *Christian* thinking is going to be confession, repentance, forgiveness, acceptance of responsibility, honesty, speaking the truth in love, and all the other peculiar virtues that are part of Christian worship.

The sermons in my collection were preached by pastors, professors, and campus ministers to students, not exclusively, but predominately young adult congregations. They thus provide a picture of one generation attempting to help another make sense of a world that has shifted on its axis. It is as yet too soon to make sure generalizations about the future course of this young adult generation. Yet I have, from my vantage in the middle of a university, a few hunches.

For some time many of us in campus ministry have lamented the civic disengagement and political apathy of our students. On our campus, the last two national elections came and went with scarcely a ripple of interest among our students. Tuesday may have thrust them into politics. Or the uncertainty, the complexity of the new world may have entirely overwhelmed them, driven them into even greater self-absorption. I don't yet know.

## The Millennial generation

Some of our students desperately want to believe that our national leaders are up to the task that is set before them, if we just give them our wholehearted support. But President Bush is my age. In my experience, this generation of young adults has little trust in my generation. In their book, *Millennials Rising: The Next Great Generation*[5], William Strauss and Neil Howe attempt to characterize America's youngest generation, those who were born after 1980 and who now populate our campuses. These veteran observers of students tell us that the best way to characterize the Millennials "is as a correction for the Boomers – that is, many of the things Boomers were not, they are."[6] These children of the children of the Sixties have tended to be sheltered, parentally protected, optimistic, perfectionistic, closely attached (via cell phones) to their parents, ultra-organized, putting a high premium on personal safety, and regarding college as a safe, well-manicured garden apart from the messiness of the world. They thus tend to embody many of the desires and values that their Boomer parents do not.

~

**What does it mean for the future of this generation that Tuesday is destined to be the defining event for their lives?**

~

Note that I have been speaking in the past tense. Reading back through Strauss and Howe's book, in preparation for this essay, I had the distinct feeling that they were describing a generation that may be in radical metamorphosis. If it is true, and I think it is, that this generation has put a high premium upon security, lack of risk, and perfect parental protection, then they were wrong. Tuesday may have rocked them in a profound way. Now, as they are called up for active military duty in a still frighteningly ill-defined war, as the economy staggers, as national leaders admit that they cannot guarantee the security of our lives or even of our mail, I expect we will witness some great changes among the Millennials. Strauss and Howe may be forced to rethink their generational generalizations, as are we all.

What does it mean for the future of this generation that Tuesday is destined to be the defining event for their lives? I recall Harvard's Arthur Levine, who has spent a lifetime studying young adults, saying that when my generation thought of "space exploration," we Boomers thought of John Glenn going up against the Russians. But when the students of the Nineties thought space, they pictured a schoolteacher being blown up in spaceship Challenger. Levine's observations suggested to me that I was not living in the same assumptive world as a student of the Nineties. What will it mean for the assumptive world of today's young adults, the "Millennials," that their definitive image will be either a huge tower cascading to earth in a hail of rubble or hate-filled terrorists dive-bombing a passenger jet into a symbol of our national pride?

Or might their emblem be courageous firefighters clawing through the rubble searching for victims? Through what lens will they look at the world?

## Supplying lenses

Any Sunday, but especially the Sunday after Tuesday, is in great part a struggle over the question, "Who gets to name what's going on in the world?" Who gets to say what is real? Through what lens, what focal image will we make sense out of the world as it presents itself to us – raw, dissonant, demanding – to be interpreted?

> As Christian preachers, we are called to read the world through the peculiar lens that is called Jesus Christ.

To be a preacher is to be one who is called by God and the church to name the world, to find the words to bring to speech what is going on. As Christian preachers, we are called to lay the gospel story over our contemporary stories, to read the world through the peculiar lens that is called Jesus Christ and his salvation. Therefore, when faced with something like September 11, 2001, we do not simply ask, "Why?" but "Why, God?"

To hear and answer to that peculiarly Christian question is both our great challenge and our great opportunity on any Sunday. God, give us the word, and then give us the courage to speak it! Amen.

## Endnotes

[1] Karl Barth, *The Word of God and the Word of Man* (1926), p. 186.

[2] Jeffrey DeYoe, "Homegrown Extremism: Preaching in Daytona Beach," *The Christian Century* (October 10, 2001), p. 7.

[3] William H. Willimon, ed., (Nashville: Abingdon Press, 2002).

[4] Karl Barth, "How My Mind Has Changed In This Decade: Part Two," *The Christian Century* (September 29, 1939), p. 684.

[5] Neil Howe and William Strauss, *Millennials Rising: The Next Great Generation* (New York: Morrow, 1991).

[6] William Strauss, interviewed by John Wesley Lowery, "The Millennials Come to Campus," *About Campus* (July-August 2001), p. 7.

# 8

# And a child shall lead them

### Bill Phipps

The vicious attacks of September 11, 2001, shattered our framework of understanding. They pushed North Americans beyond known boundaries of politics, terror, justice, and even faith.

Boundaries should be an opportunity for growth and insight. After Lois Wilson was elected moderator of The United Church of Canada, she traveled to India. She wrote of her experience in the plane:

> I peer out of the window for my first view of desert
> Wave after wave of sand
> Barren wastes with one thin track
> Stretching beyond the horizon
> Not a living thing, plant, animal, or person…
>
> How did the Wise Men ever get through from the East
> To Bethlehem?
> The preacher on Sunday said
> "Wise men aren't necessarily from the east.
> Wise men and women are those that cross boundaries."
>
> Perhaps that's why God saw fit to seat me
> Beside the Indian girl from Nairobi
> And opposite the Muslim.
>
> To see if I could.
>
> Cross boundaries, I mean.[1]

Since the autumn of 2001, we have had to cross many boundaries. We have had to come to grips with new realities. As a society, and perhaps as a world, this crossing of boundaries has challenged our conventional frames of reference.

We do not like to cross boundaries. They show us a part of globalization that we do not want to face. We evidently like open borders (so-called free trade) that allow corporations to roam the world at will and bring us cheap goods. But the fear and terror experienced by hundreds of people each day, we do not want.

## The other face of globalization

As I mourn the death of people in New York, Washington, and Afghanistan, I remember also the goat herders of Sudan whom I met, and who described the slaughter of their people, the burning of their villages, part of the two million civilians killed by a terrorist government. I sat with people in the bush, hearing stories of the firebombing of their villages and the indiscriminate slaughter of their people.

> ~
> North America, has become part of a global reality experienced every day from Rwanda to Palestine and Israel, from Sudan to Colombia.
> ~

These people, and others like them around the world, live with such terror every day. North America, in the most vicious and cruel of ways, has become part of a global reality experienced every day from Rwanda to Palestine and Israel, from Sudan to Colombia.

The infuriating part of trying to understand and act with integrity, morality, and wisdom in the face of such horror is the lack of meaningful leadership. There is little recognition of the complex mixture of fundamentalism, oil interests, Palestine/Israel, global economic disparity, and the pervasiveness of evil – and not only on one side or one location.

The hypocrisy is astounding. For decades, the United States has trained and supported terrorists throughout the world. The U.S. refuses to acknowledge international law or tribunals and draws the whole world into its vortex of "might is right." It cancels the Anti-Ballistic Missile Treaty while placing a $200 billion contract for new fighter planes.

But I hear not a word of remorse for the killing of Afghan civilians, who had no involvement in either planning or executing any attacks on North America.

Yet to raise any question or seek to probe the complexities in order to understand and act morally, one is labeled anti-American and "on the side of terrorism," as President George W. Bush repeatedly reminds us.

Since September 11, 2001, we have been engulfed by the language of war and by simplistic predictable responses by government leaders. Although there have been some thoughtful and vigorous alternative voices, they have been drowned out by politicians and media wrapping themselves in the American flag and dutifully falling in line with predictable vengeance.

> Although there have been some thoughtful and vigorous alternative voices, they have been drowned out by politicians and media wrapping themselves in the American flag.

Those of us who have the temerity to disagree with the current responses are labelled as either traitors or naïve. When we state clearly that the perpetrators must be brought to justice and held accountable for their despicable acts, we are ignored. If there is naïveté, I submit that it is in believing that waging endless war and spending billions of dollars on questionable security measures will result in peace and security.

The first casualty of war is truth. This was evident as both sides pumped up their propaganda machines. Dalton Camp wrote, shortly before his death: "In such endeavour, critical judgement becomes consumed in patriotism while being terminally suspended."

There is little or no critique in the usual sources. Despite the valiant effort of a few journalists and a few political voices crying in the wilderness, most people seem uninterested in understanding what is happening and what is at stake. Supposedly, we went to war to defend democracy. Yet our parliament did not even meet to debate one of the most serious issues of the decade, until most of the decisions had already been taken.

Not long after September 11, this headline appeared in my local paper: "We Can't Afford to Forget the Symbols of War." I am still waiting for a headline to say, "We Can't Afford to Forget the Symbols of Peace."

Vengeance can only reap vengeance.

## Addressing the causes of terrorism

What is security, anyway? The U.S. shut down Congress and postal systems because of the anthrax scare. But more people died of polluted water in one small town, Walkerton, Ontario, than in the whole of the U.S. from anthrax. We seem perfectly capable of poisoning ourselves without any help from anonymous terrorists. Doesn't any real security depend on well-educated, healthy, economically secure and pollution-free citizens who can think and act responsibly?

Doesn't the security of the world rest in addressing the *causes* of terrorism?

The former U.S. Ambassador for Counter-Terrorism, Philip Wilcox, wrote in the *New York Review of Books* that terror cannot be eliminated until its root causes are addressed.

Similarly, the front page of the *Catholic New Times* stated, "Healing for our world will not be found in efforts to get even, but rather in efforts to root out the causes of violence and plant the seeds of justice."

A *Globe and Mail* editorial said, "Whenever a new terrorist horror occurs, we are urged to look at the root causes and examine our own responsibilities for them."

These root causes are many and varied. I want to draw attention to a few forgotten, or perhaps deliberately neglected, facts:

- September 11 is not just the anniversary of the attacks on the World

Trade Center. On the same date in 1973, the CIA and its friends staged a coup to oust the democratically elected government of Chile, killing the country's president in the violent takeover. They installed, instead, General Pinochet, a brutal dictator, now indicted for War Crimes in the murder of at least 10,000 civilians.

- Ten years ago in the Gulf War, about 200,000 Iraqis were killed. Since then, about one million civilians, half of them children, have died as a result of economic embargoes and continued bombing by U.S. and British air forces.

- Senator Douglas Roche, one of the most highly respected leaders on Parliament Hill, stated in the *Catholic New Times:* "What has the war produced for us so far? In the 20th century, at least 110 million people were killed in 250 wars, six times as many deaths as in the 19th century. In the year 2000, 40 armed conflicts were fought in 35 countries. There are 500 million small arms in circulation around the world, which kill 500,000 persons a year. Governments plead that they have little money for social programs, yet they are currently spending $800 billion a year on military expenditures, which is 80 times more than they spend on the entire United Nations system."[2]

## Distorted media perceptions

Carolyn, my wife, received an e-mail message from an American Methodist minister working in Jerusalem, who was disturbed that the image the media gave us of the Palestinians after the September attack was of joy. The image was unfair. She was emphatic that the vast majority of people were shocked, dismayed, and praying for the families of the victims of the attack.

She told this story: "When we left the Cathedral after the service, we passed the American consulate in East Jerusalem. Gathered there were about 30 Palestinian Muslim girls with their teachers. Looking grief-stricken, they held their bouquets of dark flowers and stood behind their rows of candles. Silently, they kept a vigil outside our consulate. No cameras captured their quiet sorrow."

Why don't the media bring us inspiring stories of peace-building, instead of war making? I think of the Women in Black. If you're old enough, you may remember Ronnie Gilbert as the female voice in the first of the great folk groups, The Weavers. She and Pete Seeger both came under investigation by Senator Joe McCarthy's Un-American Activities Committee in the paranoia of the 1950s.

∼

**Why don't the media bring us inspiring stories of peace-building, instead of war making?**

∼

After September 11, Ronnie came under investigation again, this time for belonging to the group called Women in Black. She describes it as "a loosely knit international network of women who vigil against violence ... Because my group is composed mostly of Jewish women, we focus on the Middle East, protesting the cycle of violence and revenge in Israel and the Palestinian territories."

For this, the FBI threatened Women in Black with a Grand Jury investigation.

And why don't we hear of the Raging Grannies, of Project Ploughshares, of numerous interfaith gatherings, of the Coalition of Women for Peace in Jerusalem?

## The battle of hope versus fear

True security and democracy require knowledge of alternatives, vigorous debate, and ethical analysis. We are not getting those from most of our mass media, which have almost universally jumped onto the patriotism bandwagon. Either they do not want true security and democracy, or they no longer understand the purpose and function of a free press.

∼

**True security and democracy require knowledge of alternatives, vigorous debate, and ethical analysis.**

∼

*Tikkun* magazine (*Tikkun* is a Hebrew word meaning to mend, to repair, to transform the world) is an exception. It offered this wisdom:

The central struggle of the post September 11 period is this: will we see the world through the prism of the terrorists? Or will we see it through the prism of goodness and generosity demonstrated by the firefighters, police, and citizens who risked their lives to save others?

It is a battle of fear versus hope. If fear wins, the world will revert to an endless battleground… The greatest security will not come through armies or counter-violence, not through revenge or hatred, but through building a world of love and open-heartedness, a world in which the recognition of the sanctity of everyone on the planet shapes every economic, political, and social institution. We choose hope over fear not only because it is more consistent with who we really are as embodiments of the sacred, but also because it is the path that will lead to the greatest security.

Real courage demands honesty, probing complexities, and genuine collective commitment to address a whole range of issues to which we continually turn a blind eye. What democracy and civilization are we fighting for when real debate in parliament is perfunctory at best, and consumers (oops, I mean "citizens") are encouraged to act like lemmings?

## Loss of leadership, loss of imagination

One of President George W. Bush's recommendations as a reaction to the September 11 attacks was to "get out there and spend!"

One of our well-intentioned charity programs sends Barbie dolls to Afghan refugee children. Have we learned nothing?

Anthropologist Margaret Mead once said: "Never doubt that a small group of thoughtful, committed citizens can change the world; indeed, it's the only thing that ever does."

It seems to me that our society, most visibly reflected in our political leaders and media commentators, is suffering from an arrested imagination. Striking back with such enormous and high-tech military power is so predictable. It was the knee-jerk response in Vietnam and Cambodia, in Iraq, in Kosovo, and now in Afghanistan. None of those interventions solved the problem of the area. Why should we expect that it will this time?

The prophet Jeremiah lived in a time of total devastation. He saw God's judgment at work, as the consequences of not following God's will, the consequences of worshipping false gods, and of neglecting the Torah's ethic of addressing poverty in the face of extreme wealth, and of not really caring about one's neighbor.

> Like the child without cynicism, Jesus invites us out of the box of predictable retaliation and of an obscene build-up of arms.

We live in a similar time. But rather than doing the predictable thing and blaming Babylon for all of Israel's ills, Jeremiah challenged the people of Judah to examine themselves. That suggestion was no more popular in those days than it is in these days.

In a time of oppressive governments, the biblical prophet Isaiah talked of new leadership governing with wisdom and integrity, where the poor will eat, where human rights will prevail, and where genuine security will characterize peace with justice. "And a little child shall lead them," he wrote.

Centuries later, Jesus was born in occupied territory, was forced to flee as a refugee, later challenged the principalities and powers of his oppressed country, and was executed by the mighty Roman Empire. At Christmas, we celebrate the birth of this baby in an obscure and smelly stable 2000 years ago because Jesus represents a new paradigm for human behavior. Rooted in the tradition of his people, as exemplified in such voices as Isaiah and Jeremiah, Jesus embodies the truth of God's dream of peace with justice. With imagination and courage, Jesus turns conventional wisdom on its ear and frees people from their frozen imaginations. He compels us afresh to listen for the voice of wisdom, justice, love, and joy.

Like the child without cynicism, Jesus invites us out of the box of predictable retaliation and of an obscene build-up of arms. It doesn't take much imagination to see what a fraction of global military spending could do to address poverty, illiteracy, AIDS, and refugee dislocation.

Yet it is precisely imagination that we lack. Christ offers us an example of holy imagination, a time to wisely reflect on the human condition. It is a time to open our hearts and minds and see what might happen when we allow "a little child to lead us" – across boundaries created by fear, greed, and racism.

### Endnotes
[1] Lois Wilson, *Like a Mighty River*, Kelowna, BC: Wood Lake Books, 1983, pp. 13-14.

[2] Douglas Roche, in *Catholic New Times*, October 7, 2001.

# North America on a couch

## Nancy Reeves

On September 11, North Americans had their complacency shattered. While almost everyone in the United States and Canada has experienced some form of loss at some time – some tragedy, some crisis, some trauma – no one living at the time had experienced a direct attack on the North American continent.

As the twin towers of the World Trade Center came crashing down, so did the assumptions and expectations of many North Americans about the purpose and meaning of life. During the months that followed, North Americans struggled to find answers. Some sought spiritual solace, returning to church. Some sought vengeance, supporting attacks on Afghanistan. Some went into depression.

I am a psychologist. Much of my work deals with grief and loss. I believe that much of what North Americans experienced during the days and months following September 11 can be understood in psychological terms of encouraging healing and growth.

## The realities of loss

Most days we encounter loss – experiences that diminish or restrict us. We read a news story about a local family whose uninsured house has burned down. We speak to a friend struggling with a cancer diagnosis. Television announces the breakdown of a cease-fire in a wartorn area of our world. All these have an effect on our emotions, thoughts, and maybe our behavior. Our feelings may range from sadness as we move through the day to a state of shock that makes it virtually impossible to accomplish planned activities. Our personal reactions and responses to loss depend more on the meaning and implications the experience has for us than to the "facts" of the loss.

All change, whether leaving mother's womb or entering grade school, carries an element of loss. As we move through this change certain thoughts, words, feelings, and behaviors prove no longer useful. Some may even be damaging to our new status. Intentionally allowing an adjustment process for loss and change is a sign of physical, psychological, spiritual, and social maturity.

This adjustment process is called grief.

Over time, we come to view a number of losses as part of life. Even repeated loss or change needs to be grieved, though, since each time the meaning and circumstances will be somewhat different, as will the needs that must be met for healing to take place. The goal of the grieving process is to integrate the loss so that we can live life in a richer, more satisfying way – because of the loss, not in spite of it.

Grieving "styles" are learned. As we grow, we watch and imitate the significant adults in our lives. The overt and covert "messages" that these adults give us about change, loss, and healing affect us. We naturally accept their style of grief as the "right" way. Hopefully, this grieving style will be healing for our personality and context. If that learned grieving style is not helpful, then a conscious, intentional change of attitudes and behaviors will enable us to find a way that better fits the person we are. Practicing our new style with the small losses of daily life allows us to use it with more familiarity during times of trauma.

The range of reactions to September 11 suggests that, as a whole, North Americans have not learned to cope with grief very well.

## Trauma

Trauma is a loss with the "volume turned way up." Trauma is loss that we do not want to acknowledge or integrate into our lives. Torture, rape, the death of a child, the destruction of our home by fire or flood – all these, we believe, should not be part of our world. A traumatic event may be anticipated, such as repeated sexual or physical abuse.

Or it may be totally unexpected, such as the terrorist attacks on the World Trade Center.

We may experience death or serious injury to people, belongings, or our earth as overwhelming. What makes it a trauma, however, is our reaction. The diagnostic manual used by mental health professionals states that the person must experience "intense fear, helplessness, or horror" associated with the event.

~

**A traumatic event frequently shatters some assumptions and beliefs we hold about the world.**

~

A traumatic event frequently shatters some assumptions and beliefs we hold about the world. A few years ago, I was called to provide trauma counseling to people in a town where a young girl had been lured into surrounding bushes during a softball game in a school playing field. She was raped and killed. Help was only a softball's throw away.

People expressed strong emotions about the girl's rape and murder, of course. However, emotions expressed by many adults about shattered assumptions and beliefs were as strong. They included,

- "I moved to this small community from a large city to take my children away from violence." (One can do things that will ensure safety.)
- "I am a member of a block parent group and always keep alert for any suspicious activity. I failed." (Training or awareness will allow us to control a situation.)
- "We were playing an innocent softball game. How could evil touch us?" ("Right" living will pay off in peace and safety. The assumption that "Bad things don't happen to good people" is very common.)
- "Where was God?" (God can, will, and should intervene directly to control a situation.)

Following the attacks of September 11, people used many different words, but their shock expressed many of the same assumptions, often implying that the "American way of life" did not deserve a terrorist response; that better training could have precluded the attacks; or that this was, in some way, evidence either of God's punishment for sin or of God's absence or impotence.

## The phases of trauma

Emergency Preparedness Canada defines a traumatic event as having three time periods. The first phase, the time of "maximal and direct effects" is called the *impact* phase. It is followed by a period of *recoil* when the original threat of danger is past. At this time, some people feel relief that the trauma is over. Others begin to let the reality sink in and actually feel more traumatized than they did during the impact phase. This period of recoil typically lasts from a few hours to a few days. In the third time period, the *post-traumatic phase*, the focus is on readjustment and may last months or years.

During the impact phase, people tend to react in three different ways.

- 12–25 percent of survivors will be "calm, cool and collected." These people are seen as the heroes, responding to the reality of the event to minimize the danger, such as directing people to safety.
- 50–75 percent of survivors will react with shock and confusion. These people act in habitual ways that do not take the gravity of the trauma into account, such as stopping to collect valuable papers when the fire alarm rings. They will, however, follow directions from the group 1 leaders.
- 10–25 percent of survivors will react more inappropriately, running back into burning buildings, keeping others from safety, becoming hysterical or aggressive.

All of these styles are in the expected range of reaction to trauma. Those graphic television images from New York showed us some from all three groups.

After the impact phase, most individuals will return to "normal" feeling, thought, and behavior patterns – if they allow themselves to, or are allowed to by others. Unfortunately, some people get "labeled" positively or negatively. Others expect that they will always react to loss or stress in the same way. These will always be heroes; those will always be helpless. This labeling can produce a new set of false assumptions – we think we now know whom to trust and whom to mistrust in a crisis.

**The heroes are never allowed to show fear or indecision in future crises.**

Why does a person find themselves in group 1, 2, or 3? Skill development, knowledge, experience, or certain personality characteristics have some influence. There are many examples, however, of unexpected reactions during traumatic events. The personal meaning of the event, and one's current physiological or psychological status and stress level that day also effect our reactions to trauma. So, the group that individuals find themselves in is not pre-determined.

The injurious effects of the trauma may resolve more quickly and cleanly than the long-term effect of the labeling. The heroes are never allowed to show fear or indecision in future crises. Their bravery and clear thinking are generalized into wisdom about all aspects of life. They may be asked for endorsements of vitamins or political parties. It is very difficult for them to enter a grieving process as that would tip them off their pedestals. If they seek to leave their labeling, the group may react with aggression.

The firefighters who attended the terrorist attacks in New York have been labeled in this way. Their pictures have regularly been in national magazines and newspapers and on television, not just in news reports, but as human interest stories. I imagine that if one firefighter does not pay alimony or receives a speeding ticket, this "story" will also be advertised with shock and horror. Our heroes are not allowed to be human. This labeling creates a duality, an "us" and "them." Dualities always do violence, in feeling, thought or action, to both sides.

People in group 2 do grieve and adjust to the trauma, but may have unresolved grief about the way they have been labeled. If they accept the label, the image of confused sheep who need a strong shepherd in crisis situations may adversely affect their self-esteem. They lack trust in the growth of their abilities and perceptions.

Group 3's may become social isolates in their community or workplace. Being labeled as dangerous or out of control in a crisis may be generalized – by the individual or by others – into a conviction that this person cannot be trusted at any time. The individual may need to resign his or her position, leave the community, or agree to be closely supervised and only given innocuous responsibilities. These people are also more likely to be used as a scapegoat, if one is needed.

To move a group or community towards healing, the dynamics of these three groups needs to be named. After explaining the process, I ask the group to consciously "fire" group 1's so that they can move into their adjustment process with support and permission. Then group 2's and 3's are invited to acknowledge their reactions during that particular crisis and shift to a stance where they can use their skills and qualities to assist the healing of the group or community.

## Unhealthy reactions to trauma

Regardless of the group individuals find themselves within, each will likely experience a physiological phenomenon called the "fight or flight response." Whenever we experience danger, our brain sends us a surge of adrenalin. Without conscious control, we react instantly to maximize our safety. During this time, we usually experience great fear.

~
**Unending anxiety is one of several reactions to trauma that do not allow healing and growth.**
~

Later, when we are no longer in the hazardous situation, we may still experience that surge of adrenalin and those same feelings of wanting to run or fight. Since there is no danger present, our emotional reaction may seem identical to the time of trauma, but it is now called anxiety. Its purpose is to remind us to stay away from threatening places, people, or situations. Once we heed this message, the anxiety can move off.

Unending anxiety, however, is one of several reactions to trauma that do not allow healing and growth. These reactions start as normal and healthy but they become "stuck." Then a pattern that is life-diminishing or life-denying develops. Other patterns are unhealthy from the beginning.

## 1. The "Fight or Flight" pattern

The fight or flight response can turn into a "protective" pattern in an attempt to control life. If flight becomes a way of being, we run and hide from ourselves, others, and God. Self-awareness and self-responsibility become threatening. We try to become invisible; we refuse to commit to relationships. We are afraid that others, particularly God, are out to get us.

A fight pattern is concerned with controlling life so that unexpected change cannot occur. Relationships become static. God is rigidly defined and then expected to act always within that definition. Other ideas or experiences are threatening and therefore always wrong.

A story of a young woman who had encountered a great deal of life's pain illustrates both fight and flight patterns.

> She was still young, but felt ancient. Too much abuse, pain, suffering. So she protected her heart by building a thick wall around it. This strategy worked until she met a man who loved her to her core. Then, at first with great dread and mistrust, she allowed her wall to slowly come down. The aridity of her existence blossomed with healing and new growth. She reconnected with herself, with others, with God.
>
> Then, he was killed. Horrendous pain, but still able to fit in her worldview. She knew of others like her. Many other women in her country grieved; for the authorities were easily threatened and tended to react with imprisonment, torture, or death. Feeling solidarity with others and engaging in the structure of her faith and culture's rituals

and traditions would keep her from returning to her old, restrictive pattern.

So she decided to help prepare his body. Seeing him one last time, she could say her goodbyes. But when she tried to do this, her worldview exploded; she panicked.

Because the stone had been rolled away... and the tomb was empty...

In her panic, she didn't hide behind a wall this time. She fought! Thinking, "If I can just get his body back, I can contain this loss," she first ran to tell her friends. Returning to the tomb, she saw angels and said to them, "They have taken away my Lord, and I do not know where they have laid him." She then looked wildly around and saw a man... In her panic she took him for the gardener.

She asked for the body of the one she loved: "Sir, if you have carried him away, tell me where you have laid him and I will take him away."

It wasn't until Jesus spoke her name, "Mary," that she could move from the edges of her being back to balance within her core – and see God.

This story from the Christian gospels, which I wrote for my forthcoming book *Found Through Loss: Healing stories from holy scriptures and everyday sacredness*, illustrates the healing power of "naming" our fears. Knowing we are loved unconditionally by God, and hopefully by other human beings, produces a security in our core, a peace that passes all understanding, that anchors us during life's storms. Richard Rohr speaks of the value of "a constituting other," a person whose love for us helps define ourselves in healthy growing terms. Self-awareness helps us understand and act on our needs more clearly.

## 2. Expensive emotions
The strong emotions we experience during and after the time of trauma assist our adjustment process. If we allow them to, these emotions

inform us of our needs and may even suggest the way to meet those needs. Anger, for example, can alert us to a justice issue, or an underlying feeling of helplessness that needs addressing. It may encourage an explosive catharsis that unfreezes us physically or psychologically. Experiencing anger is useful and natural; we then choose how to act out this emotion. When we allow an emotion to inform us and then act on that information, that emotion has done its job and moves off.

The pattern I call "expensive emotions" involves attempting to protect ourselves, consciously or subconsciously, by expressing or acting on emotions for destructive or life-diminishing purposes.

There are two ways this happens. The first involves an attitude of judgment or fear about one or more emotions. We attempt to deny and suppress them. The result, taking anger as an example, produces an internal festering and transformation into a bitterness which poisons the individual's life and relationships. The second way involves treating anger as an armor and permanent response to loss. The anger is transformed into hate and vengeance.

**Expensive emotions are life-denying, keeping us from healing and growth.**

Other expensive emotions are envy, jealousy, shame, resentment, unhealthy guilt, despair, and a feeling of powerlessness. All cost a great deal in energy and time, so there is none left for healing and life-enhancement. Expensive emotions are life-denying, keeping us from healing and growth. The pattern of experiencing and acting on expensive emotions gives the illusion of power and protection because it is so visible and extreme. It creates a very intense and narrow view of the world. Expensive emotions encourage action, but that action is always towards violence in thought, word, or deed.

However, this pattern of expensive emotions is not usually identified as a choice. Grievers justify the violence of their reactions by saying that it is a "natural" outcome of the situation, or that they were "overcome" by the emotions and therefore refuse to take responsibility.

~
## The ultimate expensive emotion is the lust for vengeance.
~

The ultimate expensive emotion is the lust for vengeance. I believe vengeance is the most seductive "drug" we have because of the strong illusion that it will protect us from further trauma and will, in fact, return us to a pre-trauma status.

Once again, the pattern of responses across the United States, following the attacks of September 11, suggest to me that a great many people are trapped in these expensive emotions. With very few exceptions, Americans demanded vengeance – physically, by bombing or warfare; economically, by sanctions; emotionally, by vandalism and social hostility.

### 3. Scapegoating – the myth of redemptive violence

A particularly common pattern of vengeance is choosing an individual or group to be a scapegoat. Although the term comes to us from the Hebrew scriptures, scapegoating is found in many cultures and religions.

A goat was chosen to "carry" the community's sins. During a solemn ritual, the priest took all of the people's sins on himself and then, placing his hands on the chosen goat's head, transferred those sins to the animal. Then the goat was chased by the whole community into the desert. The violence done to the goat was viewed as sacred violence, redemptive violence, because it resulted in lifting from individuals the burden of guilt that caused estrangement and disintegration within the community. The "escaping goat" (scapegoat) ritual, invested with full sacred and legal authority, "freed" the people from sin and guilt.

During and after a traumatic event, we are in a state of high anxiety. Scapegoating shifts the blame or responsibility to another person, religion, or culture. This feels like a way to take control and reduce our anxiety. Selective chronicling of this legitimized violence ensures that the resulting history of the event focuses on the beneficial outcome of community stability and peace.

We may scapegoat consciously, or we succumb to the subconscious psychological dynamic that Rene Girard calls the "mimetic desire." Gil Bailie, in *Violence Unveiled: Humanity at the Crossroads* explores this "predilection for falling under the influence of desires – positive or negative, adulatory or accusatory – of others" (p. 51).

For example, remember a time when you went into a store to buy something specific, like a bar of soap. On your way to the soap department you passed a table of expensive "widgets," which did not interest you in the slightest. Returning with your soap you discovered an excited group around the widget table – grabbing the objects and dashing off to the checkout counter. Mimetic desire kicked in and, before you knew it, you were the proud owner of an expensive widget. You had purchased something you didn't want or need solely because of others' interest.

> ∼
> **A traumatized group of individuals quickly become a scapegoating mob when one of them suggests placing the blame for the crisis on someone else.**
> ∼

When the mimetic desire wears off we can either admit the reality and accept responsibility for a poor choice, or we can stay with the unreality and pretend that we chose the widget for its inherent value. Likewise, we either "awaken" to our scapegoating with horror, or "justify" it by calling it a needful and legitimate use of violence, or even the will of God.

Human scapegoating and sacrifice have often been viewed as divine will even though, as Bailie reports, every prophet in the Hebrew scriptures speaks out against it. Repeatedly the prophets, speaking for God, ask each member of the community to sacrifice to God their broken hearts which will allow a personal transformation for healing and growth. Repeatedly the people close their ears and give God a scapegoat instead.

Because it is so infectious, scapegoating does not need to be learned or practiced. A traumatized group of individuals quickly become a scapegoating mob when one of them suggests placing the blame for the crisis on someone else. The designated victim is quickly stereotyped, losing personal identity. Anything that would give the victim a voice and let them be seen outside of the stereotype is simply deleted from memory. Thus, after the destruction of the World Trade towers, Muslims in many North American communities were stereotyped as terrorists and endured physical and verbal violence. Even young children were not exempt.

### 4. Post-traumatic stress disorder

The initial symptoms of post-traumatic stress disorder (P.T.S.D.) are natural reactions to trauma. In most cases, individuals find the symptoms diminishing and disappearing within a month of the trauma. When instead of diminishing, the symptoms become stronger, P.T.S.D. is frequently diagnosed. (These symptoms are taken from *DSM 4R* – the *Diagnostic and Statistical Manual of Mental Disorders*, Fourth Revision.)

Symptoms of P.T.S.D. fall into three categories.

The first includes re-experiencing the traumatic event through distressing dreams of the trauma; recurrent and distressing thoughts frequently experienced as a "movie" playing in the mind that cannot be stopped; feeling as if the trauma were recurring; and intense psychological and physiological distress at people, objects, or situations that remind the person of the trauma. These distressing symptoms may occur many times during the day and night.

The second category includes symptoms that attempt to control the first symptoms. Consciously and subconsciously, the person avoids anything associated with the trauma; refuses to think, feel, or speak about it; shows diminished interest or participation in significant activities; has psychogenic amnesia – a blocking of some memories of the trauma; feels detachment or estrangement from others, a restricted range of emotions, and a sense that life will be cut short or will never be safe or satisfying again.

The third category are persistent feelings of increased arousal, such as hypervigilance, difficulty sleeping or staying asleep, irritability or outbursts of anger, difficulty concentrating, and an exaggerated startle response.

If P.T.S.D. is suspected, it should be treated by a mental health professional who is trained in desensitizing the intrusive symptoms. Sometimes people with P.T.S.D. seek spiritual directors or pastoral counselors to help them reconnect with God, or they enter psychoanalysis to look for root causes of the distress. It is a mistake to view the disorder as having either a spiritual cause or a family origin.

In my clinical experience, I have frequently found P.T.S.D. to develop in individuals who are used to viewing themselves as being in control of life. When a trauma occurs, when they discover that are not able to control the uncontrollable, the result is deep shame and a feeling of failure.

## Healing trauma

I began this chapter by identifying how assumptions can be shattered when a trauma is experienced. Consciously examining shattered assumptions, and developing new beliefs that take reality into account, will make for a more satisfying life. So often we live in myth rather than in truth. Gil Bailie says that the Greek word for truth is *aletheia* which means "to stop forgetting." Memories of traumatic experiences are often highly selective, seeing the world or a past event in rigid, black and white terms.

~
**A common assumption is that with the right knowledge and skills we can control our lives and our world.**
~

### Control vs. being in charge

A common assumption is that with the right knowledge and skills we can control our lives and our world. Even with contrary evidence staring us in the face, of how we diminish or harm when we try to control, our goal after a trauma is often to find ways of ensuring it never happens again.

Control implies direct contact and influence on a person, object, or situation. I often invite clients to deliberately control their breathing while they continue to listen or talk to me. They quickly realize that this controlling leaves them no energy or attention for listening or speaking. Needing to be in control is always exclusive. It often needs to become more and more violent to prevent other "wild" events from taking place. We frequently link the need to be in control with our self-esteem or self-image. If we are not in control, we view ourselves as weak, or failures. You may know of folks who tie their competency as gardeners to having a completely weed free lawn. They will spend an exorbitant amount of time and money and may even adversely affect or destroy other plant, animal and even human life to achieve their goal.

On the other hand, the attitude of being in charge allows for a little direct and much indirect influence. Being in charge, rather than in control, of my breathing means letting it alone most of the time; trusting it to do its job. When changes in my respiration indicate a need for more stimulation or relaxation, I can then, briefly take control and slow or deepen my breathes. An attitude of being in charge means that, rather than trying to "go it alone," I expect and welcome the influence of others, including God, in any given situation. Being in charge is inclusive and moves us towards cherishing and learning from all of creation. It encourages response-ability.

## Good grief

Clarifying the grieving style we learned as children will provide a better understanding about changes necessary to make it more healing. Allowing ourselves to grieve the small losses in our daily lives will develop a healthy pattern that is easier to implement during times of trauma. Developing self-care strategies that take physical, emotional, mental, and spiritual dimensions into consideration will give us resources that meet specific needs. Having a number of tools in only one dimension, such as aerobic activity, massage, and bubble baths will likely help our bodies through relaxation or stimulation. But these activities may have little or no effect on emotional or spiritual anguish. A range of helping strategies in all dimensions is most effective.

My book *A Path Through Loss: A guide to writing your healing and growth* gives much more information about the grieving process and helping strategies that are particularly effective in dealing with trauma, including working with guilt, setting goals in grief, and developing rituals to structure the process.

There is no doubt in my mind that Americans have been experiencing grief. I do not believe, however, that the solution recommended by President George W. Bush – to go shopping – is the best way to work through that grief.

## Symbols

I have already mentioned how the symbol of the scapegoat can be an unhealthy attempt to control the effects of a traumatic event. Other symbols can be utilized for true healing and growth.

As an example, a woman named Tara came to me for trauma counseling. She said her symbol for the grieving process was "beating my head against a brick wall." We talked about how life-denying that image was. Tara was defining the psychological, physical, and spiritual pain of grief as unhealthy and naturally trying to stop it.

With a new awareness that pain in the grieving process was healthy, and could in fact inform her of her needs, Tara was willing to develop a new symbol. She choose to view grief as a path through a dark, winter-deadened forest. As she walked along, Tara got caught on the brambles hanging over the path and was tripped by the stones and ruts. "In order to move towards healing, I need to walk the path," Tara said. "I have a choice, though, to walk it naked and suffer more pain or accept the 'padded clothing' of support offered by my family, friends, professionals, my own inner resources, and my faith tradition. It is hard for me to reach out for support, or even to accept it when it is offered. In the last few days, however, when my grieving intensified, I would ask myself if I were padded enough. If the answer was no, I would clarify the type of support that would be more effective and then ask for it. Also, with the increased 'padding' I don't need to concentrate on my feet. I can look ahead on the path and realize there is a sunny meadow in the distance."

Tara's new symbol took the reality of pain into account. It also included the promise of hope.

> ∼
> **I encourage people to consciously explore the symbols that that they use to describe their lives and then to change them as needed to encourage healing.**
> ∼

I encourage people to consciously explore the symbols that that they use to describe their lives and then to change them as needed to encourage healing. These symbols may represent the trauma itself, the process of adjustment, the healing goal, or the individual's self-image.

Regrettably, many of the public symbols emerging from September 11 seem unhealthy and self-destroying. They range from associating turbans with evil to labeling people who do not fly a national flag on their car or home as unpatriotic.

### Spirituality

Spiritual needs and practices often change as a result of trauma. If we view spirituality as an unchanging force in our lives, this change will be threatening. One woman told me how ashamed she was of herself since experiencing her trauma: "I'm not praying properly anymore."

> ∼
> **Spiritual needs and practices often change as a result of trauma.**
> ∼

When I asked for clarification, she related her usual mode of individual prayer, moving from praise to thanksgiving to intercessions. Currently, in her grieving process, she began with praise and then "the timer rings to tell me it's time to go to work and I realize how I haven't got past the first section." Even the bit of "praise" she did was not satisfying – she was saying it by rote. "So, I'm a failure in prayer," she reported sadly. At my suggestion, she was able to leave this mythic label and see *aletheia*, the total experience. This allowed her to "remember the blank period of prayer" as the peace and comfort of resting in "a loving Parent's arms."

Corporate worship may be too stimulating at first for someone feeling very vulnerable in their grief. Other people need to know that crying, difficulty concentrating, or other symptoms of grief will be accepted.

An intentional process of spiritual discernment will also help on the path of healing after trauma. In her book, *Listening Spirituality*, Quaker Patricia Loring describes spiritual discernment as "that fallible, intuitive gift we use in attempting to discriminate the course to which we are personally led by God in a given situation, from our other impulses and from the generalized judgments of conscience" (p. 12).

Discerning divine will is simple. If we can clarify our deepest need at any one moment, that is also what God wants for us. It is simple, yet never easy. Judgmental voices from our past and present, and societal "shoulds" often drown out the "still, small voice" of God. In my study of spiritual discernment concepts and methods of many faith traditions (published in *I'd Say Yes God, If I Knew What You Wanted*) I saw a number of themes.

Three prerequisites help discernment. They include having an intentional spiritual path with spiritual practices; self-awareness to help separate the voice of Spirit from the voice of ego; and right living with ourselves, with others, and with our world. A number of qualities also assist discernment, such as receptivity, patience, trust, and a willingness to use our talents and skills as co-creators with the Holy. Also, knowing how we have been guided to make effective healthy decisions in the past may show us discernment methods that will help during crisis.

## Conclusion

Most people have at least one time of trauma in their lives. No belief or action will prevent this occurring. But we do have the ability to choose a response that leads to life-affirming patterns of feelings, thoughts, and behaviors.

### Bibliography

American Psychiatric Association. *Diagnostic and Statistical Manual of Mental Disorders*, Fourth Edition. Washington, DC, American Psychiatric Association, 1994.

Bailie, Gil. *Violence Unveiled: Humanity at the Crossroads*. NY: The Crossroad Publishing Company 1995.

Emergency Preparedness Canada

Loring, Patricia. *Listening Spirituality*, vol. 1 Washington: Openings Press 1997.

Reeves, Nancy. *A Path Through Loss: A guide to writing your healing and growth.* Kelowna: Northstone 2001.

——*I'd Say Yes God, If I Knew What You Wanted.* Kelowna: Northstone 2001.

Rohr, Richard. *New Great Themes of Scripture* (audiotapes) "The perennial mistake: Vengeance and victims." Ohio: Saint Anthony Messenger Press 1999.

# 10

# The Path of Peacemaking

## Jim Wallis

I visited Ground Zero in New York City a few months after September 11. "Awestruck" was the only word that came to mind, seeing the scope of the devastation at what was once the World Trade Center on the Lower West Side of Manhattan. Thanks to the good graces of local clergy and the Red Cross, I was able to get right onto the site. The pictures I'd seen couldn't fully capture the enormity of the destruction that stood before me. Standing on the pile, I prayed and wondered what might come out of this incredible and atrocious event.

I met people doing extraordinary things that day, but I was especially struck with several groups of firefighters from cities around the country and from Canada. They had come to attend memorial services and "just to be here," as one young fireman told me. After speaking to several of these men and women, I realized what was going on. They were pilgrims visiting a holy site. That's what their faces and voices revealed to me. I've been to other holy sites and seen other pilgrims, and now saw the same thing going on at the site of the attacks.

We don't visit holy sites just for the ritual; we go to be changed. How will the events of September 11 change us? Will they change us? I am coming to believe that this tragedy could either become a doorway to transformation – or could set us back for years.

## A difficult time for peacemakers

The past year has been a difficult time for Christian peacemakers, for those of us who believe that following Jesus leads us to the path of nonviolence. Despite the great challenges to that commitment since the terrorist attacks, I still identify myself as a Christian peacemaker. But since September 11, I think we have to go deeper in that commitment.

I've been part of the peace movement for more than three decades. But the U.S. government's "war on terrorism" presents far more difficult challenges than the other wars and interventions I've fought against. In those other wars – declared and otherwise, from Vietnam to Central America, from Chile to the Congo – there was no worthy goal to be pursued, and any notion of "defending" America was nothing but propaganda.

~
**Our postmodern and politically correct world has a hard time naming evil, but Christians shouldn't.**
~

In fact, I believe that most American foreign policy since World War II has been wrong. In the name of anti-communism, the United States violated its professed values by backing a succession of ugly regimes that killed tens of thousands of their own people, trampling on every human right we hold dear. Our government backed the wrong people in South Africa until the very end. We have never really stood up for Palestinian rights against our ally Israel, and we made the Persian Gulf safe not for democracy but for our own oil interests. For 50 years, U.S. nuclear weapons policy has been based on a willingness to exterminate hundreds of millions of people. U.S. weapons sales have fueled conflicts around the world. Under both Republican and Democratic presidents, U.S. foreign policy has been morally flawed at its core.

That's what I believe, and I've protested it with 20 arrests in 30 years, all for nonviolent civil disobedience.

But the current challenge is much more complicated. The terrorists murdered almost 4,000 people in one day, and they did so with a cruel intentionality. That those people were civilians mattered nothing to the mass murderers. While President Bush's morally simplistic "good vs. evil" rhetoric is unacceptable – America has hardly been "good," given the above litany of grievances – an inability to see the stark face of evil in the events of September 11 is a moral failure. Our postmodern and politically correct world has a hard time naming evil, but Christians shouldn't. This was a horrific crime against humanity.

## Two paths

Two paths continue to emerge in response to the terror that was visited upon us.

One speaks the language and spirit of justice and invokes the rule of law in promising to bring the perpetrators of terrorist acts to accountability. Those who so violated the standards of civilized life and the human values we hold most dear must never be allowed to escape judgment and punishment, and the danger of even more terror must be urgently prevented.

The other path uses the language of war and invokes a spirit of retribution and even vengeance – emotions we can all understand. A "war on terrorism" summons up the strength and resolve to stop these horrific acts and prevent their cancerous spread. But war language fails to provide moral and practical boundaries for that response.

> ∼
> **A rising sentiment in the country wants our nation's response to be born of our best selves, and not our worst impulses.**
> ∼

Americans have seldom seen up close or felt the pain that comes from the deliberate destruction of innocent life on such a scale. Until now, it has only been in foreign lands where we have observed the horrible loss that accompanies the massive and violent rending of families and relationships in unspeakable events. Now we understand what many people who inhabit this planet with us have been forced to live with.

But it is just that collective experience of terrible pain that should help shape our continuing response. A rising sentiment in the country wants our nation's response to be born of our best selves, and not our worst impulses. We are hearing more voices asserting that we must not become the evil we loathe in our response to it, and that we should respond out of our deepest values, not out of the standards of the terrorists.

Our response will be a "test of our national character," according to a statement titled "Deny Them Their Victory," released last September and signed by more than 4,000 religious leaders. It is, indeed, the victory of the terrorists that must be denied. They and what they represent must be soundly defeated. But the question is, how? The religious leaders said, "We can deny them their victory by refusing to submit to a world created in their image... We must not allow this terror to drive us away from being the people God has called us to be." They demand that those "responsible for these utterly evil acts be found and brought to justice," but insist "we must not, out of anger and vengeance, indiscriminately retaliate in ways that bring on even more loss of innocent life."

That conviction is motivated not only by moral considerations but also by pragmatic concerns. Discipline, patience, and perseverance in vanquishing the networks, assets, and capabilities of violent terrorists is a path more likely to be effective than merely cathartic retaliation. An even more courageous national commitment would be to face honestly the grievances and injustices that breed rage and vengeance and are continually exploited by terrorists to recruit the angry and desperate.

## Telling the truth

American religious communities must take on the prophetic role of answering why this happened or, as many have put the question, "Why are so many people angry at us?" It is a challenge that will require our best discernment and a genuine soul-searching.

It is impossible to comprehend adequately the terrorist attack of September 11 without a deeper understanding of the grievances and injustices felt by millions of people around the world. That is a painful subject that the U.S. government refuses to engage, that the mainstream media avoids, and that many Americans were unable to hear during a time of mourning, grief, and anger. Indeed, the discussion has the potential to further divide, hurt, and blame ordinary people who already feel very vulnerable and under attack.

But if the conversation can illuminate the confusion many feel, it could actually help in the necessary process of national healing and offer practical guidance for preventing such atrocities in the future. Now is the time to have the courage to face this difficult question. President Abraham Lincoln, unlike most American presidents, pushed the nation to look at its own sins in a time of crisis, to dig deep into our spiritual selves and ask whether we are on God's side, rather than the other way around. We need a Lincolnesque quality of self-examination in this moment.

In our task of going to the roots of global terrorism, at least three things are important.

FIRST, in the necessary prophetic ministry of telling the truth about American global dominance and its consequences, let us never even come close to implying that America – including the victims of the attacks and their families – deserved that day of evil as some kind of judgment for our national sins, as was suggested by critics from both the Right and the Left.

> No cause, not even a just cause, can make legitimate the killing of innocent civilians.

In a powerful statement released last September by Palestinian poets, writers, intellectuals, and political leaders – who all have deep grievances with American foreign policy in the Middle East – the line was drawn: "No cause, not even a just cause, can make legitimate the killing of innocent civilians, no matter how long the list of accusations and the register of grievances. Terror never paves the way to justice, but leads down a short path to hell."

Their statement was called "But then, nothing, nothing justifies terrorism," which serves as a fitting final sentence in any discussion about all the injustice that lies behind terrorist acts. We must draw that same line.

SECOND, we must not make the mistake of thinking that these terrorists are somehow freedom fighters who went too far. On the contrary, the people that the evidence points to are not out to redress the injustices of the world. The Al-Qaeda network of terror would simply create great new oppressions, as was evidenced by the Taliban, the regime that represented their vision for the future. Their terror is not about correcting the great global gulf between haves and have-nots, about the lack of even-handed Middle East policies, or about the absence of democratic freedoms in corrupt Gulf states.

The terrorists don't want Saudi Arabia to respect human rights, but to be more like the Taliban regime – under which girls couldn't go to school, acid was thrown on the faces of women without head covers, and any religion or lifestyle different from their fanatical extremism was exterminated. For these terrorists, the only "just" solution for the Middle East and the whole Arab world is to expel all Jews and Christians. And their willingness, even eagerness, to inflict weapons of mass destruction on whole populations is beyond dispute.

The root of the terror attacks is not a yearning for economic justice for the poor and oppressed of the world. It is rather a radical rejection of the values of liberty, equality, democracy, and human rights that we take to be universal. It is the ambition of a perverted religious fundamentalism for regional and global power. However far the United States has fallen short of its professed values, and has often even contradicted them by its policies, this terrorism is an attack on those values themselves; it is not violence done to uphold or restore those values.

We are accustomed to thinking in political and economic terms. This time, we need to shift and understand motivations that are more ideological and theological. The evil of the Al-Qaeda network of terror may have been foolishly strengthened by the support of the CIA during the Cold War, but this evil is not a creation of American power. Indeed, to suggest, as some on the Left have done, that this terrorism is an "understandable consequence of U.S. imperialism" is a grave mistake of both moral and political analysis. The terror of bin Laden's Al-Qaeda network is less a reaction to an "American empire" than the radical assertion of an ambitious new empire.

THIRD, we must carefully distinguish between seeing global injustice as the cause of terrorism, and understanding such injustice as the breeding and recruiting ground for terrorism. Grinding and dehumanizing poverty, hopelessness, and desperation clearly fuel the armies of terror, but a more ideological and fanatical agenda is its driving force.

Therefore, the goal of global justice as a response to terrorism should be seen not as an accommodation, surrender, or even negotiation with the perpetrators of horrific evil. It is rather an attack on their ability to recruit and subvert the wounded and angry for their hideous purposes, as well as being the right thing to do. Evidence shows that when the prospects for peace appeared more hopeful in the Middle East, the ability of terrorist groups operating in the region was greatly diminished. We must drain the swamps of injustice that breed the mosquitoes of terror and find a way to make this a teachable moment rather than merely a blame game.

> **We must carefully distinguish between seeing global injustice as the cause of terrorism, and understanding such injustice as the breeding and recruiting ground for terrorism.**

## Learning more about our world

Despite the reputation some American travelers overseas have earned for arrogance and insensitivity, many people around the world combine a deep affection for individual Americans while still feeling a real antipathy toward the policies of the U.S. government. If ordinary Americans are to find a deeper understanding of "why so many people are angry at us," we will need to overcome our appalling ignorance of world geography and international events and develop a much deeper comprehension of what the American government is doing in our name.

Practically speaking, one idea for our response to the terrorism of Al-Qaeda might be this: Even if the multinational effort now underway limits its campaign (as it should) to successfully rooting out the networks of terrorism, that will not be enough. To be a real international effort against terrorism, the multinational effort must demonstrate a new compassion, generosity of spirit, and commitment to justice precisely toward those people who have been abandoned and abused.

Yes, let us stop Al-Qaeda's plans to hurt more people. But let us also undertake a massive and collective effort for major economic reconstruction of Afghanistan. Such a dramatic and public initiative would clearly demonstrate the relationship between halting terrorism and removing injustice. Suffering people everywhere would see the clear signal, and the recruiters of pain would be dealt a death blow.

It's time for justice – for the perpetrators of terror and for the people whom our global order has, for so long, left out and behind. How we respond to these murderous events will shape our future even more than the terrorists can.

## How shall we respond?

Although I've opposed the language and tactics of war in the campaign against terrorism, the task of preventing further terrorist violence against innocent people is a worthy goal, and the self-defense of Americans and other people is clearly at stake here. If there is a good – and even necessary – purpose in defeating terrorism, and if the lives of my neighbors and my family are indeed at risk, how do I respond?

> They would destroy democracy, deny human rights, repress women, and persecute people of other faiths – and even those of their own religion who disagree with them.

Terrorists use and manipulate American global injustices to justify their crimes and to recruit the angry and desperate for their violent purposes. They have no interest in the global justice and peace that many of us have lived and fought for – indeed, they are its enemies. Their vision for the world is absolutely oppressive. They would destroy democracy, deny human rights, repress women, and persecute people of other faiths – and even those of their own religion who disagree with them. Even worse, they blaspheme the name of God by doing their violent work in the name of religion. To dismiss them as merely Islamic fundamentalists or marginal extremists is not enough; these terrorists are educated, well-financed, and coldly calculating ideologues who will quickly and massively kill whenever it suits their clear purpose – which is to take power over Islam and the entire Muslim world.

We must be realistic and confront the fact that terrorists are even now planning further violence against innocent people, on as massive a scale as their weapons and capacities will allow. They are people who seem not to be bound by conscience or limits on the destruction they seek.

> For nonviolence to be credible, it must answer the questions that violence purports to answer, but in a better way.

So how do we stop them? How do we prevent them from killing more innocents? And most poignantly, how do advocates of nonviolence try to stop them? For nonviolence to be credible, it must answer the questions that violence purports to answer, but in a better way. I oppose a widening war that bombs more people and countries, recruiting even more terrorists, and fueling an unending cycle of violence. But those who oppose bombing must have an alternative.

I've advocated the mobilization of the most extensive international and diplomatic pressure the world has ever seen against Al-Qaeda and other networks of terror – focusing the whole world's political will, intelligence, security, legal action, and police enforcement against terrorism. The international community must dry up the terrorists' financial networks, isolate them politically, discredit them before an international tribunal, and expose the ugly brutality behind their terror.

But when the international community has spoken, caught the terrorists, tried them and found them guilty, and authorized their apprehension and incarceration, we will still have to confront the ethical dilemmas involved in enforcing those measures. The terrorists must be found, captured, and stopped. This involves using some kind of force.

To accept any use of force is a very difficult thing for those of us committed to nonviolent solutions. Is any kind of force consistent with nonviolence? If so, what kind? What limitations are required? What ethical considerations must be brought to bear?

Over the last year, I've talked with a wide range of Christian peacemakers. Some are delving into Dietrich Bonhoeffer's painful decision, as a pacifist, to join the plot to assassinate Hitler. Others are rereading French theologian Jacques Ellul, who explained his decision to support the resistance movement against Nazism by appealing to the "necessity of violence" but wasn't willing to call such recourse "Christian." Many are going back to Gandhi and asking what he meant when he said that nonviolent resistance is the best thing, but that violent resistance to evil is better than no resistance at all.

> To accept any use of force is a very difficult thing for those of us committed to nonviolent solutions.

Some believe that there can be no resistance to terrorism, either because of the sins of American foreign policy or because of their principled pacifism. Others are only willing to deal with "root causes" while continuing to oppose the American foreign policy that, in their view, is behind this terrorism. They point out that the United States has been guilty itself of sponsoring or supporting "state terrorism" – a painful reality I've observed most recently in the Palestinian West Bank and Gaza, occupied by Israeli defense forces.

But like many practitioners of Christian peacemaking, I can't accept such a non-response to horrific terrorism, regardless of the history of U.S. foreign policy. Gandhi said that if a lunatic is loose in the village and threatening the people, you first deal with the lunatic, and then with his lunacy. I believe we must find a way to deal with the threat of terrorism – a threat that must not be avoided or minimized by those committed to nonviolence. We cannot turn away from this. But how do we confront this crisis?

## Exploring the meaning of peacemaking

The "just war" theory has been used – and abused – to justify far too many of our wars. This crisis should not turn us to the just war theory, but rather to a deeper consideration of what peacemaking means.

In the modern world of warfare, where far more civilians die than soldiers, war has become ethically obsolete as a way of resolving humankind's inevitable conflicts. Indeed, the number of people, projects, and institutions experimenting in nonviolent methods of conflict resolution has been growing steadily over the past decade with some promising results.

I am increasingly convinced that the way forward may be found in the wisdom gained in the practice of conflict resolution and the energy of a faith-based commitment to peacemaking. For example, most advocates of nonviolence, even pacifists, support the role of police in protecting people in their neighborhoods. Perhaps it is time to explore a theology for global police forces, including ethics for the use of internationally sanctioned enforcement – precisely as an alternative to war.

> War has become ethically obsolete as a way of resolving humankind's inevitable conflicts.

Mennonite theologian John Howard Yoder was engaged in that task. He was asking whether those committed to nonviolence might support the kind of necessary force utilized by police, because it is (or is designed to be) more constrained, controlled, and circumscribed by the rule of law than is the violence of war, which knows few real boundaries. If that is true for the function of domestic police, might it be extrapolated to an international police force acting with the multinational authorization of international law? Yoder's work in this area was never completed, but perhaps now it should be. I recently heard New Testament theologian Tom Wright provocatively suggest that the ethics for global policing possibly might be extrapolated from Romans 13.

Theologian Stanley Hauerwas, author of the seminal *The Peaceable Kingdom* and other works, says, "I just don't feel like I've found a voice about all this yet." Hauerwas doesn't like it when people tell pacifists to "just shut up and sit down" during a time like this. He believes that pacifists cannot be expected to have easy policy answers for difficult political situations that are often created, in part, by not listening to the voices of nonviolence in the first place. Nevertheless, he believes the advocates of nonviolence can and should offer alternatives that reduce the violence in any conflict. As a professor of ethics, he is quite willing to call governments to observe the principles of a "just war," such as the recognition that soldiers killing each other is morally preferable to soldiers murdering civilians. And Hauerwas favors the use of international courts and global police to resolve conflicts. But he doesn't agree with the conventional wisdom that says "The world changed on September 11." Hauerwas says, "No, the world changed in 33 A.D. The question is how to narrate what happened on September 11 in light of what happened in 33 A.D."

> The "myth of redemptive violence" is again being used to try to prove to us how violence can save us.

Walter Wink, a biblical scholar at Auburn Theological Seminary, offers a crucial critique of how – in the war against terrorism – the "myth of redemptive violence" is again being used to try to prove to us how violence can save us. He remains convinced that it cannot. Nonetheless, he admits to being glad when the "bad guys" lost in Afghanistan and women, among others, were liberated from Taliban tyranny. He too would greatly prefer the course of international law and police. We simply haven't trained the churches, or anybody else for that matter, in the crucial theology and practice of active nonviolence, says Wink. That must now become our priority.

Wink would no doubt agree with the approach of Fuller Theological Seminary professor Glen Stassen, who speaks convincingly of the "transforming initiatives" that can be taken to reduce violence in any situation of conflict. Exploring what practical nonviolent initiatives can be undertaken to open up new possibilities is more important to Stassen than merely reiterating that one doesn't believe in violence.

John Paul Lederach, who teaches at the University of Notre Dame and Eastern Mennonite University, is perhaps doing more to open up those possibilities than any other contemporary Christian thinker or practitioner of nonviolence. In this terrorism crisis, he has many creative insights into how a network like bin Laden's might be defanged and defeated without bombing an entire country. In particular, Lederach speaks of the need to form "new alliances" with those closest to the "inside" of a violent situation. In this case, he feels that Islamic fundamentalists who don't share the terrorists' commitment to violence might be the most instrumental group in defeating them. Undermining violence from within, Lederach feels, can often be more effective than attacking it from without.

Christians must continue to defend the innocent from military reprisal, prevent a dangerous and wider war, and oppose the unilateralism of superpowers. But we must also help stop networks of violence, and the threat they pose to everything we love and value. All that presents difficult questions for peacemakers, but it is a challenge we dare not turn away from.

No one has all the answers. Humility is a good trait for Christian peacemakers, while self-righteousness is both spiritually inappropriate and politically self-defeating. This much is clear: Jesus calls us to be peace-makers, not just peace-lovers. That will inevitably call us to face hard questions with no easy answers. In the end, Christian peacemaking is more a path than a position.

## Overcome darkness with light

Lighting candles at prayer vigils is something many of us have done more times than we can remember. Speaking the language of darkness and light at interfaith services, in liturgical seasons, and in the streets has become a matter of habit. But our darkness has felt very real and powerful this past year – almost impenetrable, and threatening to close in on us. And our need for the light feels most urgent.

Old familiar spiritual words must take on a new reality for us now, and a new sense of mission. Words like "Let there be light!" and "A light shines in the darkness, and the darkness has not overcome it." But we must not just light candles. We must make a new commitment.

More than we knew before September 11, there are many dark places in the world where terrorist violence against large numbers of innocent people is being planned. Those places must be exposed to the light of day and the violence be thwarted. There also are dark places within us, and in our nation, that might lash out from our deep woundedness, grief, and anger, carelessly inflicting more pain on innocent people. The light of compassion and reason must prevent us from spreading our pain.

**Courage is not the absence of fear, but the resistance to it.**

We need the light of courage to face the darkness that lies so thick and heavy before us – courage to heal the darkness in ourselves; courage to reveal the darkness in the very structure of our world; and courage to confront the darkness in the face of evil. Courage is not the absence of fear, but the resistance to it. In these days, we need to light candles and make commitments so that the darkness will not overcome the light.

# CONTRIBUTOR BIOGRAPHIES

CHAPTER 1– **DEREK EVANS** is currently Director of the Naramata Centre, a United Church of Canada retreat and leadership training center. He was formerly Deputy Secretary General of Amnesty International. Prior to that he served as Executive Director of the Canada-Asia Working Group, a research and policy institute of the Canadian Council of Churches.

CHAPTER 2 – **STANLEY HAUERWAS** is Gilbert T. Rowe Professor of Theological Ethics at Duke Divinity School where he has been on faculty since 1984. He delivered the prestigious Gifford Lectureship at the University of St. Andrews, Scotland in 2001. The same year, *Time* magazine named him America's Best Theologian. He is the author of 25 books.

CHAPTER 3 – **WALTER WINK** is Professor of Biblical Interpretation at Auburn Theological Seminary in New York City. He is the author of 250 articles and 14 books, including a trilogy on the Powers, and, most recently, *The Human Being: Jesus and the Enigma of the Son of the Man.*

CHAPTER 4 – **JAMES TAYLOR** co-founded Wood Lake Books publishing house and is a former managing editor of The United Church of Canada *Observer* magazine. He has written several thousand magazine articles and newspaper columns, and is the author of 13 books, including *Everyday Psalms*. Portions of this chapter were excerpted from *SIN: A new understanding of virtue and vice.*

CHAPTER 5 – **LOIS WILSON** was the first woman Moderator of The United Church of Canada. She is a past president of the World Council of Churches and of the Canadian Council of Churches. She currently serves as a Senator in the Canadian Senate. She is the author of several books, including two on women of the Bible: *Miriam, Mary and Me* and *Stories Seldom Told.*

CHAPTER **6 – KEITH WRIGHT** served for 40 years as pastor in the Presbyterian Church U.S.A. He received a Doctor of Ministry degree and the Distinguished Alumni Award from Austin Presbyterian Theological Seminary, Austin, TX. He is the author of *Religious Abuse: A pastor explores the many ways religion can hurt as well as heal.*

CHAPTER **7 – WILLIAM WILLIMON** has been Dean of the Chapel and Professor of Christian Ministry at Duke University, Durham, North Carolina since 1984. His articles have appeared in many publications; he is Editor-at-Large for *The Christian Century.* His *Pulpit Resource* is used each week by over 8,000 pastors in the U.S.A., Canada, and Australia.

CHAPTER **8 – BILL PHIPPS,** minister of Scarboro United Church in Calgary, Alberta, is a former Moderator of The United Church of Canada who has also worked as a poverty lawyer, community organizer, hospital chaplain, and adult educator. He was for ten years Executive Secretary of the United Church of Canada's Alberta and Northwest Conference, where he took particular interest in native and aboriginal concerns.

CHAPTER **9 – NANCY REEVES** is a clinical psychologist, psychotherapist, spiritual director, poet, and author of two books, *A Path Through Loss* and *I'd Say Yes, God, If I Knew What You Wanted.* She is director of the Island Loss Clinic in Victoria, BC, and teaches at the University of Victoria.

CHAPTER **10 – JIM WALLIS** co-founded the Sojourners community in Washington, DC, and has been editor of *Sojourners* magazine for more than 30 years. (Portions of this chapter were compiled from articles published in *Sojourners.*) He is convener of Call to Renewal, a national federation of churches, denominations, and faith-based organizations working to overcome poverty. His most recent book is *Faith Works: Lessons from the Life of an Activist Preacher.*